HOW TO COPE WITH SPLITTING UP

VERA PEIFFER was born in 1953 in West Germany and moved to London in 1982. After obtaining a degree in psychology, she became interested in hypnotherapy and completed diplomas with the International Association of Hypnoanalysts (IAH) and the Atkinson-Ball College of Hypnotherapy (ABCH).

Vera now runs a private practice as an analytical hypnotherapist in Ealing, west London. She also teaches stress management at the London Business School and runs Positive Thinking workshops.

Overcoming Common Problems Series

Overcoming Common Problems Series

Overcoming Common Problems Series

Overcoming Common Problems

HOW TO COPE
WITH SPLITTING UP

Vera Peiffer

SHELDON PRESS
LONDON

First published in Great Britain 1991
Sheldon Press, SPCK, Marylebone Road, London NW1 4DU

© Vera Peiffer 1991

British Library Cataloguing in Publication Data
Peiffer, Vera
   How to cope with splitting up. – (Overcoming common problems).
   1. Couples. Separation. Psychological aspects
   I. Title   II. Series
   155.643

ISBN 0–85969–625–1

Photoset by Deltatype Ltd, Ellesmere Port, Cheshire
Printed in Great Britain by
Courier International Ltd, Tiptree, Essex

*In memory of Arminius Wald,
the only person who never
needed this book.*

Contents

Introduction

Aren't relationships difficult? Two years ago you met this man and he was wonderful, witty and entertaining and interested in everything you did. Now you look at him across the dinner table and you realize that he is probably never going to go on holiday with you and that his mates will always come first. You don't really have anything in common and it appears that it is only the physical side of the relationship that keeps you together, and this is not really your idea of happiness and a fulfilling partner-ship . . . .

You are a professional woman and financially independent, you are reasonably attractive and this is not the first relationship you have ever had, which means that it is unlikely that it is going to be the last. So why is it that the thought of leaving him frightens you?

Splitting up is, without a doubt, one of the most traumatic events in a woman's life, and it does not really matter whether you leave him or he leaves you: the separation is bound to have emotional repercussions for both sides. Once the honeymoon-period is over and the clay feet start to show (both yours and his), it does not make any difference whether you are married to him or not: if the problems cannot be solved in a satisfactory way for both sides, the relationship will eventually fail.

Today there are more women earning their own living than there were ever before in history, and that means that women have a more realistic choice between getting married or main-taining a more independent lifestyle. Having their own job enables women to provide for themselves, and as a consequence, marriage is no longer a financial necessity. This material independence has made new forms of relationships possible where the partners either just live together without being married, or where both parties retain their individual homes while they are going out with one another.

This tendency towards 'freer' partnership arrangements does not mean, however, that women do not want relationships. On

1

the contrary, relationships, and especially an intimate relationship with one particular partner, are still one of the top priorities in a woman's life, no matter how emancipated she is or how high up the career ladder. But although greater financial independence makes it less pressing to stay in an unsatisfactory relationship, there still exists a conflict. On the one hand, an independent woman can afford to have higher expectations of her partner, but on the other hand there is still an emotional component that often seems to put the brake on walking out on a partner who does not measure up to your standards.

In the following chapters we shall look into the reasons that lie at the bottom of this seemingly irrational reluctance to break free from a relationship even though we are unhappy in it.

This book discusses what happens when these more informal variations of partnership break up. In spite of the greater freedom these types of relationship provide, their break-up can be just as traumatic at that of a marriage. Once emotional links have been forged, splitting up causes distress, no matter how many difficulties and problems marred the relationship in the past. Some people are so frightened of the emotional consequences of a break-up that they prefer to continue in an unsatisfactory relationship rather than give it up; others will make the break but then take years to recover from the effects.

Even more traumatic is when you are the one left by your partner, especially when it seems to happen suddenly, with no prior indications that things were not working out between you. The famous example where he just pops out to get a packet of cigarettes and never comes back is probably the worst that can happen, closely followed by finding a note on the kitchen table or a letter on the doormat to say that he does not want to continue seeing you for one reason or another. The feelings of shock, disbelief, anger and grief that you are left with after announcements like that are not dissimilar to those you experience when someone close to you dies.

It is important to be aware and understand the mental and emotional processes you are going through before, during and after the split-up because the more you know about these processes the better you can work out strategies to alleviate their negative effects. It is a fact that most of us will at one time or another be faced with a partnership situation where things do not work out despite attempts to rescue the relationship, and we need to be able to cope with such a situation without letting it shatter our life for years to come.

In my practice as hypnotherapist/psychoanalyst I see a great number of people who suffer from depression and lack of self-confidence as a direct result of having gone through the break-up of a relationship. As the clients work through their problems and begin to gain a new and more positive perspective again, their confidence and happiness return.

A lot of confusion arises during and after a split-up through a mixture of seemingly contradictory feelings and negative emotions, and it can appear to be a mammoth task to disentangle them. This book will help you to recognize more clearly the processes that unfold as you go through the various phases of separating.

We have greater influence on the outcome of a break-up than we think, and it is well worth our while to contemplate using our energy in a positive sense to help us through the difficulties during and after a break-up. Splitting up does not have to be a disaster; how well you cope with it is very much under your control. Even though different personalities react in different ways, there are nevertheless predictable similarities between people; so look at the solutions this book offers and put them into practice, and you will not only deal more successfully with your situation, but you will also come out at the other end a happier and more competent person.

1

Difficulties in Relationships

Any relationship will at some stage go through a rough patch. This is part and parcel of being close to another person. Provided the foundation is solid and there is good communication between the partners, difficulties can usually be resolved, and as a consequence, the relationship grows stronger and closer.

In the following chapters you will find descriptions of some of the most common difficulties that can occur in relationships and which can (but don't have to) lead to a rift that is severe enough to bring about a split-up.

As you are reading through the various examples, you may find parallels to problems you are experiencing or have experienced in your own relationship with your partner. Please remember that you will still have to decide for yourself what you want to do about these problems. If you feel the relationship is worth saving, then the following chapters will help you become more aware of the different facets of the problem, and this in turn will enable you to tackle them more constructively. If, however, you feel the relationship is past repair, you will have to make a move to disengage yourself from your partner.

Incompatibility

Opposites attract – or do they? There are various reasons why people with opposing personalities and conflicting views will get together, and the following are some examples for each case to illustrate the point.

'I adore you'

Peter had fallen in love with Sharon – madly in love. She seemed the most wonderful creature in the world to him. He told all his friends about her and finally plucked up enough courage to ask her out. He was overjoyed when she accepted. They started going out and Peter was in seventh heaven; he finally had the woman of his dreams! She did not seem to have a lot of time for him and could only see him once a week, but Peter didn't mind. She also made derogatory remarks about his friends and Peter himself, but he took this as being her particular sense of humour; surely she didn't mean it. He began to think seriously about marriage, and even when friends told him that they had seen Sharon with another man, Peter ignored the warnings. He decided it would be an insult to Sharon to even ask her to comment on these rumours. To Peter, it was impossible to contemplate that Sharon could have any faults or shortcomings.

Two months later she left him for another man. Peter was heartbroken and unable to understand why she had broken off their relationship all of a sudden. . . .

Peter's case may be an extreme example, but it is by no means an uncommon one. For some people, being in love has the disturbing side-effect of anaesthetizing the rational mind to an extent where the person floats through life on autopilot, hypnotized by the object of their desire. They do not really see the other person, they only see what they want to see; they are in love with a figment of their imagination. They will neither see nor admit that their love is one-sided because they automatically ignore any signals that do not fit into their concept of adoration. Even when incompatibilities are pointed out to them, they will sweep them under the carpet or reinterpret them into an acceptable version, finding all sorts of excuses to explain unpleasant behaviour with which their partner confronts them. This is a bit like doing a jigsaw puzzle and cutting the pieces with a pair of scissors to make them fit – you will never get the true picture.

'Marriage will change everything'

You may be quite aware of some major differences between you and your partner but still think that you can bring about change through the power of your feelings for the other person. This is an idea that often precedes the wish to get married. Even though there are things between you that don't work out you think that by getting married you will feel better, your love will get stronger and therefore your partner will change or you will be able to adapt better to the things you could not cope with in the past. Let me give you an example.

Veronica had been married to John for two years and she was beginning to be very unhappy with certain aspects of their relationship. John's job involved a great deal of socializing in the evenings, and Veronica was asked to come along to most of the events, which she did. Veronica found it easy to talk to other people and enjoyed going to these functions; the only thing that marred her pleasure was the way John behaved when in company. Usually he was a friendly and retiring man, but as soon as they were at a party or an official function, he became noisy and always tried to be the centre of attention, oblivious of the fact that he often interrupted others or intruded on private conversations. He appeared self-opinionated and always had to have the last word.

This was, however, not a new thing. John had been like that ever since Veronica had known him, and it had always bothered her. She had attempted to point it out to John, without success. He dismissed the issue, insisting that Veronica was overreacting and that he certainly had not had any complaints from anyone else. There had been frequent rows about this issue before their marriage, but Veronica had been hoping that their new status as husband and wife would alleviate tensions and either make John a calmer and more considerate person or give her the poise she needed to put up with his behaviour in a more gracious manner.

None of this happened. John continued to be noisy at social gatherings and Veronica grew more and more disgruntled. She felt embarrassed whenever she had to go out with her husband and started avoiding it. In the end, this rift proved to be irreparable.

Why is it we think that marriage will work a sudden miracle on our shortcomings? We still seem to hold this curious image of marriage as a magical cure-all, the answer to all our interpersonal problems, when really this is quite an unrealistic view when we look at it in a detached manner.

Marriage puts stress on a relationship because it is a commitment, and if you are serious about your marriage vows, it is a commitment for life. Even though outwardly nothing may change (you may have lived together before anyway), saying 'I will' changes things emotionally for you. Who can honestly say that they were entirely untroubled by thoughts like, 'What if this is all a big mistake?' during the time leading up to the wedding?

Emotional stress can be caused by negative events but also by positive ones, and whatever category you will want to put 'marriage' under, the fact remains that it puts you under pressure. Everything that was a problem before marriage is therefore likely to become a *more serious* problem after marriage because when you are under emotional stress you find it more difficult to cope with problems. If things are seriously wrong during the courting period while both partners are still on their best behaviour, it is highly unlikely that the problems will vanish after marriage.

'I need you'

Opposite personalities will also be attracted to each other when the partners complement one another in their weaknesses. You can, for example, have a constellation where one person is timid and helpless and the other person has a tendency to tell others what to do. When two personalities like that get together, they often form a strong initial attachment because each of them gets what they need: the timid person gets relief from anxiety because they finally have someone who makes all their decisions for them, and the domineering person can dominate and feel needed.

Another combination of opposing personalities is the lazy person and the workaholic, where the workaholic cannot stop busying themselves with all sorts of chores and tasks, feeling needed and important in the process, and the lazy person pursuing their favourite pastime, namely doing nothing.

On first sight, these 'odd' couples seem to be ideally matched, but as time goes by, circumstances change and people change, and one of the partners may overcome their weakness and outgrow their partner, and all of a sudden, the other person is no longer needed.

Sonja had never been very happy at home. Her father was strict, her mother overprotective. Sonja had been longing to leave home for a long time, and the great day finally came after a year at university. She managed to convince her parents that commuting to and from university took up too much time, and her parents finally agreed to let her rent a bedsit near the campus.

Sonja finally had what she wanted, but after the first euphoria had worn off she began to realize that she was now faced with another difficulty: she did not know how to live in the outside world. She had never learned how to handle money, how to make decisions for herself and how to deal with being by herself. She was frightened and getting more and more nervous which made her even less capable of dealing with all the new challenges that came her way, until, much to her relief, David appeared on the scene. He was kind and understanding and told her not to worry, he was going to look after her. He took troublesome decisions off her hands, redecorated her little bedsit for her and filled her evenings.

Sonja was blissfully happy; everything seemed to be going her way, and the relationship became a steady one. She finally moved in with David. With his help, she became more competent and gradually lost her fear of problematic situations. As she grew more confident, she needed David less and less. She had started developing away from David, and he could not adapt to the new status quo. He still wanted to tell her how to do things, but now Sonja did not want to follow his advice any more. She felt she had become a person in her own right and wanted to make her own decisions. After three years, the relationship broke off.

'Look at me – I'm interesting'

This is something that happens often at the beginning of a relationship where one or both of the partners transform into miracles of wit, sagacity and eloquence. They confess to loving the theatre, opera, ballet, cinema, art galleries and so on; in other words, they are culture vultures *par excellence*. They might even end up taking you to the cinema once or twice, until the first euphoria has worn off and the true person comes out from behind the glamour veneer. It's a bit like Superman, only the other way around: you see him in his blue and red hero outfit *first* and then he goes into a phonebox and turns around three times, sparks flying, and you are left with a meek and un-adventurous little man who likes to spend his Sunday afternoons in front of the television watching cricket.

This initial display of initiative and vivacity may even be quite genuine and is not necessarily meant to purposely deceive the other person. It is simply born out of a feeling of happy excitement at going into a new and promising relationship. The only problem with this is that it is only temporary, and if you have picked your partner because you saw him as being compatible with you, sharing your love for going out and doing things that do not involve the television set, then it can be a major disappointment when you find that your prince has turned into a frog after you have kissed him a few times. You are then left with the options of either continuing to make your own entertainment by going out with friends or going out by yourself, but it is still frustrating if you would have preferred to go out with your partner.

This type of incompatibility is easily overcome when *both* partners have been exaggerating their culture-mania a little and things even themselves out for both of them at the same time. Often, the mere fact that you are in a steady relationship tends to have a sedating effect on both, and with the arrival of children, outside entertainment has to be curtailed anyway so that through the shift of priorities the focus of attention revolves more around domestic life.

Affairs

Affairs usually happen when a relationship is out of balance, and this can occur for a variety of reasons. During periods when the relationship is going through a rough patch it is more likely that one of the partners will have a fling than at times when the relationship is running satisfactorily for both sides. If one of the partners is unhappy with a particular aspect of the relationship, for example the lack of physical or emotional closeness, and when the topic has been brought out into the open and *still* nothing changes, there is a possibility that this partner will give in to temptation when the opportunity offers itself, either responding to or making advances to a third person in the hope that this liaison will provide the intimacy they need.

A lack of physical and emotional closeness in a relationship creates loneliness and feelings of frustration, simply because you do not feel wanted. If you are never touched or stroked or cuddled you feel left out and unloved, and it does not make any difference whether you are two years old or sixty-two. Friendly physical contact is a basic human need that needs to be fulfilled. Walking arm in arm, holding hands, sitting close together on the sofa every once in a while is essential for your wellbeing because these gestures act as confirmation that you are welcome and accepted. If these boosters are absent or very infrequent, you begin to feel neglected and discontent, and even though you may not purposely go out and look for someone else, you are certainly more susceptible to attentions that are shown to you.

The escape into an affair can also be caused by jealousy. If one of the partners constantly suspects and accuses the other one of infidelity, this can ultimately lead to a self-fulfilling prophecy where the accused finally goes out and does what he or she has been accused of – at least they won't be getting a hard time at home for nothing!

Jealousy has nothing to do with love. It is a bottomless pit which you can fill with love and reassurance and devotion until doomsday and it will still not make the slightest difference because your partner will still doubt your loyalty. Jealousy is born out of a deep-rooted feeling of insecurity and unworthiness, usually coupled with a tendency to promiscuity. The jealous person often feels quite all right about their own philandering tendencies ('It's nothing serious . . .') but will not allow their partner the same kind of freedom; double standards *par excellence*!

Lastly there are the so-called open relationships where the partners have agreed not to tie one another down and make affairs part of the relationship, but this tends to work out for short times only, if at all. Whereas in the beginning, the partners may think that their love for one another is strong enough to stomach each other's occasional affairs, they eventually find out that what in theory sounds like a good idea is very hard to put up with in reality. But rather than change the rules they set initially and that so obviously don't work, a sequence of tit-for-tat ensues where the ultimate aim is to hurt the other person more than they have hurt you. It is an illusion to believe that rational agreements about sexual freedom will translate into emotional acceptance when it comes to the crunch.

Affairs are a recipe for disaster. They destroy trust and intimacy, and even with the greatest of goodwill it takes a long time to pick up the pieces again, but more often than not they destroy the relationship.

Violence

'If he only as much as raised his hand to hit me, I'd be off like a shot!' – Most women find the idea of physical violence in a relationship so appalling that they cannot imagine wanting to remain with a partner if he hit them – and yet many women do.

The extent of physical abuse ranges from pushing and shoving to regular beatings and attacks with weapons like knives. These outbursts can be sparked off by a real or imagined mistake the woman has made, for example not having his dinner ready on time, or it can come about because the man has had trouble at work or is under some other form of stress. Alcohol usually aggravates the outbursts, although it is not the main trigger for violence.

Violent men can have two very different sides to them. They may, on the one hand, be very charming and persuasive if they put their mind to it, and they may have other positive sides to them; and yet they harbour strong feelings of disdain and hatred for women. These men usually come from a family background with a weak father and a domineering mother.

Women who stay with such men tend to come from a background where they were treated without respect, and often also beaten, so that they just exchange one abusive environment with another when they go into a relationship with a man. This is the only way they know life to be, and this is why many battered women go back to their abusive husbands, lovers or boyfriends. Often, violent men can be extremely persuasive when they see that their partner is serious about leaving them. They will beg, plead and vow eternal love, just to keep the woman from walking out on them. They may even mean it when they promise that it won't happen again, but unfortunately, this type of violent behaviour is well out of rational control, so unless the man gets professional psychological help with his problem, it is unlikely to be resolved.

If the man refuses to seek professional help, there is no other option for the woman but to leave the relationship, but this is often easier said than done. Much depends on how badly the woman's self-confidence has been undermined and how much she has been convinced (or convinced herself) that it is her own fault that he beats her. Feelings of guilt and shame prevent many women taking that final step and walking out, even though physical abuse tends to get worse as time goes by. Some women will fabricate the most fantastic lies about how they contracted that black eye or that bruised arm, rather than admit that their boyfriend or husband inflicted it.

As long as the woman stays around, however, the beatings continue. It is an illusion to believe that one can sit it out and that it will get better one day. Experience shows that it *won't*. In a relationship where there is physical violence it is imperative for the woman to leave and begin to build up confidence and self-esteem, either with the aid of self-help groups or through psychotherapy. The only way to avoid making that same mistake again, namely getting involved with an abusive partner, is to strengthen your ability to stand on your own two feet. Learning to respect yourself will help you attract men who will respect you.

Growing apart

It is difficult to detect the initial processes that make you drift away from your partner, which is why it may come as a surprise when you are suddenly faced with the fact that you have grown apart. There is nothing wrong with going out to see your friends separately or pursuing different sports and pastimes. On the contrary, it keeps the relationship interesting if you have things to talk about that you did *not* do together; so this is not the problem. Doing things separately only becomes a problem when one or both partners start building their own world to the exclusion of the other, if there are two separate worlds which do not overlap sufficiently.

This process of drifting apart can happen to love relationships just as much as to friendships, and maybe it is those partners that don't live together who are most prone to encounter this difficulty because of the physical distance they impose on one another, which, in a way, is like saying 'I want to keep my own world for the time being'. In such a situation it is imperative that there be mutual interests (not just sex) that form a link between the couple, and this link has to be solid enough to form an emotional bond; otherwise it is only too easy to drift back into one's own, readymade world, away from the other person.

This is not to say that couples who live together need not worry about losing touch with one another. Living together is by no means a guarantee that it won't happen to you. On the contrary, living together forms a safe base from which to operate and explore the outside world, it constitutes a stable background for an ambitious career, both for men *and* for women, and it is only too easy to neglect the partner over your own professional plans. If striving for a career or indulging in a hobby ultimately takes over everything else, at the expense of the relationship, the partners will no longer have anything in common. It then all depends on whether there is enough love or liking between the couple to make them stop in their tracks and attend to one another when they come to realize what is happening. It is not so much a matter of whether love has priority over career/pastime, although many couples behave as if it were ('You can choose: it's either me or your Sunday football matches!'). The point is that you need to find an acceptable balance that incorporates your partner in a way that is satisfactory to both. This admittedly takes time and effort, but the fact that you are sitting down together and discussing what you can do about the situation demonstrates that you are interested in the relationship and that you are prepared to do something to keep it going.

Growing stale

Again, not an easy one to detect until you are confronted with the tatters of the relationship. It creeps up on you, that sense of boredom and fatigue, that crisp-crunching frustration of another Monday evening slouched in front of the television set, too bored to talk to one another, too lazy to do anything else.

As a rule of thumb you can say that if you are bored with life you are bored with yourself. It is easy to abdicate responsibility and blame your partner for being unimaginative and a stick-in-the-mud, when really your partner is not there to entertain you and keep you amused. What happened to the activities you used to do together, the things you used to enjoy? Have they all and sundry fallen prey to everyday humdrum routines?

When you start going out with someone it seems the most natural thing in the world to want to spend as much time as possible together and to do lots of things together, and this works admirably as long as the relationship is new and exciting. Once both partners are settled and get more used to one another, doing things together becomes even better because you feel comfortable and relaxed in the presence of the other person and you can therefore enjoy your mutual activities more. So far so good. When, however, you lose interest in what you are doing but still continue with it because it has become a standard routine, you are entering the twilight-zone of zombie-dom. Granted, routines have a reassuring quality and they are safe boundaries within which you feel protected. But even though the home you created with your partner appears to be your castle, it can turn into your prison if these boundaries are not expanded every once in a while. Where the need for security is so great that changes cannot be tolerated and constitute a threat to your emotional balance, inertia sets in and, with it, boredom.

Harmless though it may appear, boredom is one of the major destroyers of relationships. Unlike affairs, which constitute an outside intrusion into a relationship, boredom destroys it from within, and even though some people are prepared to accept this as a price they pay for being in a relationship ('A boring relationship is better than no relationship at all!'), many do not, but then the question arises: what is worse, a relationship that has lost its lustre or the struggle to get out of it? If there is nothing to complain about, no major shortcoming in the partner, how do you explain that you want out? And so the tug-of-war begins between knowing you should discuss with your partner ways of breathing new life into the relationship and, on the other hand, the prospect of it all being in vain, anyway. Depending on the personalities involved, attempts at reviving the relationship can be very successful. However, if one partner refuses to cooperate because he/she feels content within the given boundaries, there is not a lot left for the other person but to face the inevitable and leave.

Non-commitment

Contrary to public belief, non-commitment is not an exclusively male trait of character, although it has to be said that, on the whole, the reticence to attach themselves emotionally seems to occur more often in men than in women.

Part of the explanation for this phenomenon may be that women are still brought up to measure their own worth in terms of how attractive they are to men. One symbol of being attractive is to find a man who will marry you – or at least go out with you, and even though women may not consciously be aware of these social undertones, they are there nevertheless and often act as driving force behind an urge to attach themselves to a more or less suitable male. Within this old male–female setup, a relationship means financial and emotional security and the end of a race against age and other female competitors. Does this sound selfish? Well, it is. For some women, having a partner is important because they want his money and status, the man being secondary in their endeavours to attach themselves.

But there are also other reasons why women seem to find it easier to commit themselves, and these reasons are rooted in the fundamental differences between the male and female psychological make-up. Women, on the whole, find it easier to express their emotions and talk about them, simply because it is socially acceptable for women to acknowledge their feelings. Men seem to be far more worried about their own emotions and the hold these emotions have over them to acknowledge them officially. Boys who want to grow into big strong men are not supposed to cry and therefore develop into men who can no longer cry. It is still more common to see women displaying grief at a funeral than men; it is still more common to see women exchanging confidences than men.

This fear of acknowledging and acting upon 'unmanly' feelings such as grief, love or tenderness may account for many a retreat from a possible relationship that threatens to become too close for comfort. Sex is all right because it blends in nicely with man's self-image as warrior and conqueror, but all the emotional extras like kissing and cuddling are confusing the issue because they bring feelings into play which he is trying to avoid. That way the relationship is kept nice and tidy, just sex but no further involvement. Does this sound selfish? Well, it is, but it is also a sign of emotional immaturity.

A man's announcement that he does not want to commit himself should be taken seriously. If you can avoid the missionary-trap ('He will change once I have slept with him', or 'He has never had anyone as wonderful as me; I'll make him change his mind!') you will save yourself a lot of heartache. This is not to say that non-committers will never change, but if their first sentence in your presence is 'Don't count on me!', it is unlikely that this will happen with you. This does not mean that you are unattractive or uninteresting, it just means that he is not ready. Don't waste your time waiting for a miracle; you are just blocking the way for someone who is seriously interested in you.

Money

Have you noticed that it is only people with stacks of money who say that money isn't all that counts. . . ? Even though we may like to think that money is of secondary importance in our lives, the truth is that it matters quite considerably whether you have it or not, and this has repercussions for a relationship just as much as for individuals.

Money causes problems mainly through its absence. At best, the lack of money prevents you from going on holiday or treating yourself to extras like a weekend away; at worst it affects your ability to pay bills or other fixed costs like mortgage or rent. Couples who live in separate flats may not feel these effects on their relationship so much, but being in dire straits *and* living under one roof can put enormous pressure on a relationship, especially when the partners have opposing views of how to handle the situation.

Debbie and Julian had been living together for a couple of years and were planning to get married in a year's time. They were both working, but they knew that they needed to save in order to pay for their honeymoon and to pay off various debts that had accrued over the last couple of years. One day as Debbie was checking their bank statement against her cheque book she found that quite a substantial sum of money had been withdrawn from the account, but not by her. When she talked to Julian about it he started making excuses but finally admitted that he had taken it out to spend on evenings out with his colleagues. Debbie was annoyed because she had been budgeting very carefully, trying not to buy anything for herself in order to pay off their debts as quickly as possible, and here was Julian, spending their money on entertainment! They had a long talk about the matter and Debbie explained that it was essential for them to be careful with their money if they wanted to manage their finances *and* have money for a honeymoon, and Julian agreed to restrict himself from now on.

Everything went well for a few months, until Debbie found that Julian had cashed another batch of cheques behind her back. Debbie felt deceived and hurt by Julian's dishonesty. It seemed almost as if he was trying to sabotage their wedding on purpose. She challenged him to tell her what had made him act in this way and made it quite clear that she was very disappointed and seriously considering leaving him should the same thing happen again. In the end, all went well and they got married. Nevertheless, their differences about money had seriously jeopardized the relationship.

Lack of money causes stress. If you have to worry about how to pay your bills every month, you are tense, you are uneasy and there is an atmosphere in the house. If this happens on a regular basis, the tension has to be discharged in one way or another, and often this happens by picking at the partner. Rows occur more frequently, angry outbursts and accusations pass your lips more easily when you are under financial pressure. When no consensus can be found how to tackle the situation, or if one of the partners refuses to pull their weight, the relationship can be seriously affected.

Sex

Similar to the issue of emotional commitment, sex is a subject where male and female needs don't always overlap. It would certainly be inaccurate to say that men's sexual needs are completely different from those of women. There are lots of women who are just as enthusiastic to make love and just as active in the process as men. The differences that exist lie more on an emotional level. Although both men and women can experience the act of lovemaking as intimate, women tend to give greater meaning to it than men. Women regard sex as an emotional investment in the relationship, and this feeling seems to be more or less absent in many men. As the relationship progresses, regular sexual activity with the partner will mean that the woman will feel more and more involved, assuming (or just hoping) that this is also the case for her partner.

Men appear to be able to detach the sexual act, if not from intimacy, but certainly from a sense of commitment. If the woman is willing to go along, they look upon it as an agreement between two consenting adults who want to have a good time together, but nothing more. So if a relationship is still fairly new, with each partner assuming that the other one understands the implications that sex has for them, they can end up disappointed or surprised when they find out that their expectations had been very different indeed.

A problem can arise when the woman does not like sex. Many women will quite willingly go through the motions of lovemaking during the initial period of the relationship, only to withdraw later more and more from it. This leaves the partner in a no-win situation. If there is a good emotional bond between them, the man will not want to leave because of her unwillingness to have sex, but he will also feel frustrated and rejected at the lack of physical love.

Successful sex is very much a question of chemistry, but also one of experience. A clumsy fumbler is unlikely to draw an inexperienced or inhibited woman out of herself, whereas an experienced woman can still have a reasonably good time in bed with a sexually not very competent man, simply because she can manipulate the situation by telling the man what she wants.

Sexual problems can put pressure on a relationship not only when women reject sex but also when men do not give their partner enough attention in the form of non-sexual physical contact, such as kissing and cuddling, which often is of higher significance to women than sex.

Neither female reluctance nor male inattention can be cured by force. Inhibitions concerning the physical side of the relationship need to be tackled from a psychological angle, just as the inability to get emotionally involved. Paradoxically, people with inhibitions tend to deny that they have a problem and will therefore not seek help. According to them it is the other person who is oversexed or overdemanding, and therefore it is the partner who should see a psychologist, not them!

The biological clock

If a woman wants children, she will not only have to find a suitable partner, but she also has to find him by a certain deadline or her chances to conceive are minimal or fraught with unreasonable risks to herself and the baby. The closer to her biological deadline the woman gets and the keener she is on starting a family, the more she sends out messages of urgency – a sure way of sending men running as fast as they can in the opposite direction, for surely, this must be the ultimate in commitment: to have a girlfriend/wife *and* a baby!

The biological clock can make a woman more clingy, more determined to win the man over, to convince him to stay with her and, if possible, marry her. As her desperation is not helping her self-confidence, women in this situation are often unwilling to split up, even though their partner is quite clear about the fact that he does not want to commit himself. By not leaving the relationship, the woman is unable to find a more suitable partner who would enable her to start a family.

The fear of being without a partner can be so great that the woman ultimately decides to stay in the relationship, despite her feelings of bitterness and resentment. Her negative feelings and the pressure she puts on her partner, however, make it more likely that he is going to leave her in the end.

2

Phase I: Decision-making

We have just looked at some of the problems that can, but do not necessarily have to, lead to the break-up of a relationship. Let us assume that you have tried everything, you have talked to your partner about the problem, you have waited, but nothing has changed and you are feeling more and more unhappy in the relationship. By that time, the thought of leaving your partner will undoubtedly have already crossed your mind once or twice, but it still seems too drastic a step to be seriously considered.

Often, this process of coming to a definite conclusion about your plan of action lies hidden for a long time and just expresses itself as a niggling doubt at the back of your mind. It can be like a thought that you don't want to acknowledge and therefore push away. Eventually, however, the issue can no longer be avoided, and it is at this point where many people start consciously procrastinating. Making a definite decision about whether or not to continue the relationship means that you will have to go and do something about it; in other words, you will have to take responsibility for your decision. People often shy away from taking the risk of making the wrong decision and then having to face the consequences, such as loneliness and guilt.

In the following I have outlined some of the issues that can keep you in this unpleasant state of limbo, and also what price you pay for being passive. *Not* making a decision is also a decision, so it doesn't really solve anything if you don't make up your mind.

Hopefully the next sections will help you become more aware of the processes that hold you back from making that final decision. As you begin to sort out the various reasons that hold you back you will be better equipped to get to grips with them.

Apathy

The facts seem to be obvious: you are rowing a lot and you, as well as your partner, are getting petty and moody. There is a

21

constant atmosphere between you. There are more bad times than good times, things have been said that should never have been said, and still you don't want to draw the consequences. Your partner may not even be aware of the possibility that you might want to leave. He tells you he loves you, but he nevertheless continues to see his parents on weekends rather than you. You are obviously not number one, and you don't like it because this is not your idea of an adult relationship. At times you get so angry that you decide the only way out is to leave him; after all there are more men where that one came from! You imagine yourself telling him this and how it would make him crumble and repent what he has done to you, but it doesn't work out like that. Next time you see him he brings you a big bunch of flowers and tells you he will try and see you on Sunday. You are pleased and relieved and, naturally, drop your separation plans for the time being. He turns up on Sunday evening at 7 pm but only stays for a couple of hours because he has to get back home – a hard day at the office awaiting him the next morning. . . .

Now you are not sure whether to be mad at him or not. After all, he has made an effort. Maybe you are too fussy? Maybe you nag too much about things that cannot be changed? Self-doubt creeps in, shaking your confidence in your decision to leave him, but soon the old feelings of disappointment and anger reappear and you are back to where you started from, until he takes you to the theatre next week. . . .

This wavering between hope and disappointment is exhausting and unproductive because it just wears you out without achieving a true improvement in the relationship. Apart from anything else you are also worried about how you will cope with being solo again should you really go through with your plan to leave him.

Fear and indecision have a paralysing effect, and this can last for a long time, sometimes years, where the relationship remains in an unsatisfactory state of limbo. The spell is usually only broken when an event occurs that is too important to be ignored.

The trigger

Resentment and anger put you under stress. As negative feelings accumulate without being resolved in a satisfactory way, your patience with your partner eventually wears thin, and the time comes where your frustration has reached a pitch where it outweighs any fears or doubts – and you walk out. This is in many respects the best way because it represents a clearcut expression that you are no longer prepared to invest in the relationship.

If you are unable to deal actively with your dissatisfaction, you run the risk of falling ill over it. Suppressed anger creates depression: the anger is turned inside instead of out. You begin to feel out of control, lose self-confidence and self-respect and generally begin to feel run down. All this means that you are even less capable of handling the flawed relationship, so you abdicate responsibility to your partner. It is now up to him to show whether he is still interested in the relationship. Is he going to look after you while you are feeling unwell? Does he care enough to make more time for you? If at this crucial time he cannot prove his love for you, then usually this will serve as the trigger for a decision to terminate the relationship. It seems that sometimes we need to see our last hopes shattered in front of our very eyes before we can allow ourselves to withdraw from a detrimental partnership.

Another way out is, of course, to get involved in another relationship. If another man appears on the scene this can serve as the final excuse to leave your partner. That way the possibility of being on your own after splitting up is elegantly avoided, at least in the short term. In reality, the other man is only a vehicle to get you out of a relationship you no longer want. He is your rescuer and private therapist who is there to help you work through all the injustices you feel you have been subjected to in your previous relationship. You may feel really grateful to him for helping you, but this is not necessarily the same thing as loving him for his own sake.

It takes time to get over a relationship; how much time will depend on the personality of the person concerned. While you are still working through your feelings for one man you are not really open or ready to dedicate your attention to the next one, which is why relationships on the rebound hardly ever work out.

What are your standards?

When a relationship starts going wrong it is important to determine for yourself what it is that bothers you and how important it is to you to set the problem right. The focus is on what you *actually* feel, not what one *should* feel. Your standards refer directly to your personal likes and dislikes and they have nothing to do with any general set of rules.

If you find it hurtful when your partner never introduces you to his friends then that is what counts. If you find it unacceptable when your partner sleeps around then that is what counts, no matter how many people tell you that it probably doesn't mean anything and all men do it at one time or another. Take your *own* feelings seriously, they are the only thing you have to go by. If a situation feels right, it *is* right; if it feels wrong, it *is* wrong.

There are certain qualities you need in your partner in order to ensure that you are happy in the relationship. Some qualities may be more important to you than others. You may be willing to negotiate or to give in on some points, but others will be so essential to you that without them you would feel out of sync with your partner.

When you deviate too much from your standards you are in danger of losing yourself. It is a sign of self-respect to expect to be treated well by your partner. Being extra-nice and putting your own wishes last, on the other hand, are a sure recipe for disaster. If you don't speak up for yourself and make sure the other person is informed about your wishes and needs, you cannot even blame your partner for ignoring them. If you don't take yourself seriously you cannot expect others to do so.

In making a decision about whether to leave your partner or not, you will have to determine what your values are. Remember that your values are neither right nor wrong, they are just yours as opposed to anyone else's. If things don't work out with your partner it is likely that some of your most important standards are not met, and if you have made the problem known and you can still not negotiate a better deal for yourself, then you are going out with the wrong man. At this stage you have the choice of either to continue being unhappy in the relationship, or to leave and be unhappy for a while but open yourself to the possibility of finding a more compatible partner. The decision is yours.

3

Phase II: The Revelation

Once you have made up your mind to leave you need to announce your decision to your partner, but many people shy away from this task. Rather than sitting down with the partner and openly talking about their wish to separate, they will try to get the message across indirectly. They are suddenly no longer available for mutual evenings out and start making excuses for not being free for weekends with the partner. This withdrawal is often preceded by a row which is brought about on purpose, giving the person who wants to leave an excuse to withdraw.

Much will depend on whether you live together or in separate places. It is easier to 'disappear' from a relationship if you have your own flat, whereas living together means that all your belongings are in his place (or vice versa) and you will have to find a new place to live once you have announced that you are going. Should your partner take the split-up badly, the time between announcement and your actual leaving could become very unpleasant indeed.

Revealing to your partner that you are about to leave or finding out that your partner wants to leave you is a matter of a few minutes' talk, but it is nevertheless the moment of greatest shock, whether the revelation comes as a surprise or not. Even if you have anticipated that your partner may not be around forever, the fact of actually being *told* that he will go is an emotional blow, and in that respect, the revelation period is the most traumatic.

You leave him

Telling someone else you don't want to stay with them any longer inflicts pain because it is a rejection and a blow to the ego. Basically you are telling the other person that there are things about him that you don't like and that these shortcomings are so grave that you prefer to be on your own or with someone else rather than with him. This is what it sounds like to your partner, even though you may not say it in so many words.

25

In order to soften the blow you may begin to talk about all his positive points. Remarks like 'You are really a very interesting person and so intelligent', or, 'You have helped me find my feet and you have been so supportive over the last two years' are meant well but, at this stage, can provoke confusion and anger in your partner, because why, if he is so wonderful, do you want to leave him? Even if you mean what you say, it doesn't sound true at the time; it sounds like you feel sorry for him (which you probably do) and try to console him out of pity. You have hurt his pride and he will therefore often reject your mollifications as dishonest. At this point in time it is bewildering rather than helpful to enumerate his virtues; it confuses the issue and raises false hopes in your partner.

In some relationships, the woman's announcement that she is going to leave results in the man totally losing his composure and showing feelings like shock, grief or despair – maybe for the first time in his life. This genuine show of emotion is bound to create a very intimate situation. You may suddenly doubt your own judgement of him and wonder whether you have not just made a big mistake. Your heart goes out to him because he is suddenly showing feelings; he may even beg you to stay. Now the confusion is complete and you really don't know what to do.

Please don't forget one thing now: this is an exceptional situation. If this is the only way you can get your man to show his feelings for you then this is not good enough. You have hopefully had a good long think about this relationship before you took the decision to split up with him, and there must be good reasons why you want to go, so stick by your decision. Things that he says in a highly emotive state may come from the heart, but they will not necessarily effect any positive changes in the relationship when things are back to normal.

The more emotionally your partner reacts to your announcement, the more likely it is that you feel guilty for what you have 'done'. Guilt is part of the process of splitting up, not just for the person who is leaving but also for the person who is left. You may feel selfish and mean, but on the other hand there is no point in continuing in a relationship that makes you unhappy. As time goes by you will be able to look back at the time with your partner and assess things more clearly, simply because you have detached yourself emotionally.

26

He leaves you

Let us look at the other side of the coin. What happens when *you* are the one who is asked to sit down for a talk, when *you* discover that *he* wants to split up?

No matter how prepared you were for something like this to happen, you will still be shocked. We all have this ability to ignore negative premonitions that don't fit into our concept of the relationship. We are aware of some of his traits that suggest that he is not quite as involved in the relationship as we would wish, but then we brush this aside, trying to focus on his other more positive points that make up for the negative ones – and we push the negative aspects into the background.

One of these negative points may very well be his inability to be emotionally intimate and committed, and you now remember how he told you in the beginning that he might not be around for good and that one day you would end up hating him, and how you dismissed his initial warnings. Now you are faced with the consequences of your own carelessness. If only you had taken his initial remarks seriously!

The initial shock is normally followed by a feeling of betrayal. You have given your best, you have worked on the relationship, made concessions, revealed your innermost being to your partner, and he just throws it away as if it all meant nothing to him. You don't want to believe that you have misjudged him so severely, but there it is, right in front of your eyes: he says he is going to leave you. Shock and bitterness are mingled with anger and fear, anger at him for hurting you, anger at yourself for not having taken his initial warning seriously, and fear of what the future will hold once he has left.

Another typical feature of the situation is a sudden drop in self-confidence. No matter how furious you are with him, there is still this small niggling doubt at the back of your mind that maybe if you were more attractive (or better educated or a better cook) he would have stayed. As in all times of crises, your self-doubts and real or imagined weaknesses now drift to the surface again and come back to haunt you, especially when you hear that he is leaving you for someone else. Immediately you start fabricating a picture in your mind of that new woman, giving her the most stunning looks, the most fabulous figure, making her into a supercook and highflying career-woman with a terrific sense of humour who is marvellous in bed, and all this in answer to your question, 'What has she got that I haven't?'

And while you spend all this time picturing the other woman as exceptionally attractive, you drag yourself further down, which in turn lowers your self-confidence even more.

The most important issue, however, is what you are going to do without him. He may have had his faults, but he was someone to go out with, to be seen with. You have in the meantime grown unaccustomed to tackling restaurants, cinemas or the theatre on your own, and you dread the idea. For some women, the prospect of being on their own again is practically unbearable, and they will feverishly go through their list of available male or female friends that could serve as escort until further notice. They also think about any men who have shown an interest in them in the past and ring them up to tell them about the split-up which, of course, is just another way of saying that they are available again and want to be comforted.

The lower the woman's self-confidence, the more likely she is to either try and get into another relationship as quickly as possible or to hang on to the man who has left her. She will ring him constantly, ask him to think it over, and beg him to come back. Unfortunately, this openly displayed dependency usually tends to alienate the partner even further rather than attract him, so that these attempts at mending the rift ultimately always fail, even though the partners may get together again temporarily. Emotional blackmail like threats of suicide will keep the situation in limbo for a while, but they are no guarantee for a continuation of the relationship. They may prolong the process of parting, but they are likely to make it into a bitter one because no one likes to be blackmailed.

As a long-term solution it is certainly better to let the other person go. That way the emotional wound is allowed to heal rather than being ripped open again and again by recurring bouts of hope that you may be able to entice him back, only to be disappointed to see that he cannot be persuaded. The sooner you can accept the fact that he is no longer willing to stay with you, the sooner you will get back on your feet again.

You hear from someone else

Rather than breaking up, some men will start seeing someone else and keep the existing relationship going at the same time. This can go on for quite a while, sometimes months or years – until someone sees him. And even then it can take time until you hear about it because it is an unpleasant message to pass on. His friends won't tell you because they are his friends; your friends may feel unsure whether they should tell you because they don't want to upset the applecart, but in the end, there is usually someone who comes forward.

Being told by someone else that your boyfriend is seeing someone else is humiliating. You feel like a fool for not having noticed that something was wrong and that you were so naïve as to believe the explanations he gave for his absences. Maybe you even refuse to believe that it is true, hoping against hope that your friend has made a mistake.

The only way to find out, of course, is to ask him, and this is difficult, whether it is true or not. If it all turns out to be a mistake you have demonstrated that you think him capable of such a thing, and if it is true, your trust in him will be badly shaken; but ask you must because you need to know where you stand.

When you tell him what you have heard, the most likely answers you will get are as follows.

'Yes, it is true, but it doesn't mean anything!'

Some men will make out that you are being hysterical about the whole matter (which you may well be by this stage) and narrow-minded and old-fashioned. They assure you that the other woman doesn't really count and that, anyway, you don't own him. If you have any self-respect you will pack your bags and go or throw him out. Someone who still needs to play the field while he is going out with you is a waste of time and obviously not ready for a serious relationship.

Don't be deterred by the labels he is giving you. They are manipulative. The only thing that counts at that moment are your feelings, and if you feel hurt about the way he is conducting himself then that is what is important, no matter whether he calls these feelings exaggerated or not.

'Yes, it is true. I was drunk. I'm sorry!'

Depending how good your relationship has been so far it may survive this aberration. Nevertheless, the fact that it happened seems to point to a problem because if the relationship is solid it should be possible to fend off temptation. So even if you stay together you need to sit down and talk to make sure any problems come out into the open so that your relationship can be put onto a more solid basis.

'No, it's not true. How can you believe such a thing?'

He denies it but your friend is quite sure. What can you do? You may want to sit back and wait to see whether more evidence comes to light; you may want to have a detective check on him; or you may decide to believe him. The fact is that it will come out one day. If your friend has made a mistake, your boyfriend should be able and willing to explain where he has been and should do so without you having to ask.

Accusing you of lack of trust *can* be a ploy to distract your attention from the real issue, and it often works because you don't want to mistrust him. On the other hand you are certainly entitled to speak to him about what your friend has told you. There is no point in keeping it all in, being devoured by jealousy and hatred, when you don't even know if it is true.

You are bound to find out whether he is having an affair or not. If you find that he is, you will have to decide whether you are happy with being one of two women in his life or whether you expect a relationship of a more committed nature. Should you feel that you cannot live with this situation you will have to leave. If you stay you are condoning his behaviour, and it is unhealthy to stay in a situation where you get hurt all the time. If you let him have his cake and eat it you are promoting your own misery. This is not the time to lower your standards. Make it clear that you are not prepared to put up with it. Move out for a while and stay at a friend's or tell him you wish to end the relationship. You are better off without him.

The great disappearance act

Even though this may be a rare event, I would like to discuss it because the disappearance act is just another way of saying 'I WANT OUT'.

There are several variations to the theme. You may come home and find that all his clothes, tapes, CDs and books have gone, and the only thing he has left is a note on the kitchen table saying something like, 'I'm sorry, I don't want to hurt you, but I feel I have overcommitted myself. I need more freedom.'

He has made a decision and carried it out, and all that without as much as consulting you. All neat and tidy for him, no drama, no scenes, no tears (or none that he has to witness), and he is out of it; a true anti-hero solution. It does not really matter what that note on the kitchen table says, whether he wants to find himself, wants to be more independent or feels unable to uphold your relationship because you cramp his style with his pals; what he means is that he is desperate to go but does not want to face you.

Don't spend too much time trying to understand his note. Any assumptions you are making are purely hypothetical because his note may not give you the true reason why he has left. His way of leavetaking indicates a lack of courage and an unwillingness to communicate which would have been detrimental to the relationship in the long run anyway. You should, however, spend some time thinking about the relationship and determine whether you have overlooked early warning signals that heralded his walkout; but more of that in Chapter 5.

If you are not living together, the disappearance act can manifest itself in the fact that he just doesn't turn up for dates anymore and that none of his friends or family seem to know where he is or what he is doing. It is as if the ground had opened and swallowed him.

You may now begin to wonder whether he has had an accident or fallen prey to a sudden loss of memory and wandering aimlessly along a deserted country road. . . . Well, these things do happen, but the likelihood that he has just walked out on you is unfortunately much greater. Even though the total-amnesia possibility would be the kinder for your ego, the I'm-off possibility is the more probable. Get someone else to ring his home or work, and if they can get hold of him, then at least you know what is going on.

If the disappearance act happens while the relationship is still in its beginnings, be glad you found out early enough to avoid further emotional upheaval. A man who cannot be bothered to tell you that this relationship is not for him is not really what you want. Don't begin to adjust your standards downwards; you owe it to yourself to look around for someone who is as serious about a partnership as you are. Be glad that you had a lucky escape, learn from your past mistakes and get happy again; this is the best strategy to find a new partner.

If the disappearance act happens after the relationship has already been established for a while, it is going to be harder to cope. Once you have settled down in the relationship and have built up trust in your partner, his withdrawal becomes doubly painful.

Sometimes the disappearance act is followed by a sudden reappearance trick, also known as rabbit-out-of-the-hat. After a period of several weeks he turns up on your doorstep, out of the blue, with a big smile on his face and a bunch of flowers in his hand, kissing you passionately, sighing deeply and launching into an explanation as to why you haven't heard from him for a month or two.

This is the time to keep your rational mind switched on at all cost. Do not allow your relief at seeing him again bamboozle you into forgetting what you have gone through during his absence. If you forget it, you will be forced to live through the experience again, because if he can do it once, he can do it again. He may even swear to you that he will change. If you believe him you'll have two chances: a fat one and a slim one. Smooth talking is unfortunately not the same thing as reliability, and if you want to retain your self-respect and protect yourself from further emotional injury you would do well to send him riding off into the sunset.

4

Phase III: Splitting Up

So now both parties know that the relationship has come to an end and the break is about to be effected. Couples who have lived together will now begin to look for separate places again, divide up their belongings and inform friends and relatives about the split-up. Even though the dramatic interpersonal part is over, there are still various practical and emotional problems that have to be overcome until everyone is finally installed in their respective new lives.

The problems that are addressed in the following do not necessarily occur in every case, but at least some of them are likely to emerge, in various degrees of intensity, depending on the personalities involved.

Practical problems

There are usually quite a few practical issues to be considered when you separate, and even though they seem to be less important than the emotional problems, they nevertheless have to be dealt with. You will see in the following examples that the issues addressed seem simple enough but can be made difficult by the emotional component that tends to pervade them.

Telling mutual friends

Splitting up with your partner can in some cases have repercussions on your circle of friends. Announcing that you are no longer with your man can get you reactions ranging from utter disbelief ('I always thought you had the *perfect* relationship!') to sympathetic pats on the back and the proffering of a box of Kleenex ('Poor lamb! How *could* he!'). You may find that some of your friends who were originally his friends, will withdraw, demonstrating that they are taking his side or that they want to stay out of it altogether and rather not see either of you.

Eileen and Alex had decided to split up. The separation took place in an amicable way, and in order to announce their parting to their friends, they had a farewell party at their mutual home before they moved into separate flats. At the party, Eileen and Alex were verbally attacked by one of their friends, Stephen, who said how disappointed he was in them for not staying together and that it was a disgrace that they parted when they had everything going for their relationship.

Outbursts like these usually come from people who are in a shaky relationship themselves, as was the case with Stephen. Seeing his friends split up made him worried about his girlfriend Silvia who had threatened several times to leave him, and he did not want Silvia to take a leaf out of Eileen and Alex's book and carry out her threat.

Another example was given to me by Susan. She said when she had split up with her boyfriend, her friend Philippa's husband became cooler towards her and started to regard her meetings with Philippa with suspicion. He knew that his marriage had been on the rocks for a long time and feared that Philippa might follow in Susan's footsteps and leave him. As it turned out, his fears were justified, and his marriage broke up not long after.

It is true to say that the splitting up of one couple can cause ripples amongst their friends and even precipitate the split-up of mutual friends – *but only if the relationship was not working anyway*. There is no way that a good relationship is affected by the fact that another couple is parting company.

Friends tend to react more sympathetically towards the person who has been left by the partner because this is considered to be the harder lot, and rightly so. But no matter how close your friends are, they will never be able to assess or understand completely what your relationship with your partner was really like because they can only judge by what they saw as your 'public' image as a couple, and they usually only hear one side of the story.

When you tell your friends about the split-up it is a good idea to try not to slag off your partner. It is over, and no amount of insulting remarks will re-establish the old times. This is not to say that you should not discuss your feelings, but that is different from verbal abuse. Keeping a tab on how you speak about events helps you to put them behind you more quickly which means you can begin to focus your energies on new, constructive goals.

Telling parents

If you have a good and open relationship with your parents you will want to let them know about the split-up, and this could cause different types of problems. Although they may respect your decision, they could still be secretly worried about what is going to become of you. They may have hoped that you were going to get married, and as the years go by they see your chances dwindle. You are thirty-eight and not even divorced, let alone married! Your market value deteriorates rapidly! And who will look after you when you are old? Well, unless you get married to a younger man, chances are that your husband won't be there to look after you anyway as men's life expectancy is about eight years shorter than that of women. . . .

Your parents may also start pointing out to you that your standards might simply be too high and you may sense doubt sneaking into your mind that they could be right and you have made demands that were too high. Don't! Your standards cannot possibly be too high. If you aim for mediocrity then that's what you will get; if you aim for excellence then that's what you will get. There is no point in lowering your standards anyway, because deep down your needs are still there and they will not go away just because you ignore them.

When your relationship with your ex-partner has been a long one you may have become friendly with his parents, and they with you. Depending on how your splitting-up took place and depending on who left whom, this friendship may continue or not. I know quite a few families that still see their son's ex-girlfriend, even though the ex-couple don't see each other any more. But it is also possible that his parents now reject you, especially if it was you who left their son. It seems a great shame that this should happen but there is not a lot you can do about it. You will have to accept that the family is closing ranks. It is their decision to do so, and they have a right to this decision just as much as you had a right to leave him. The sooner you can accept it the quicker you can get onto your feet again.

Separating possessions

Even though the separating of possessions looks like a formality on the surface, it can have heavy emotional undertones, especially when the split-up is less than amicable. Fighting over that vase or that armchair you bought together can translate into, 'Well, if you don't want to live with me any longer, at least I'll make sure I take you for everything you've got!'; in other words, we are talking revenge here. This can escalate to an extent where a partner insists on having a clock which you know he positively hates, just to get back at you.

When both of you are stubborn, the process of who should have what can extend over weeks and months. It is nearly as if by holding on to the mutual possessions you are holding on to the relationship, with the only difference that now you hate your partner whereas before you loved him.

In some cases the battle over possessions brings the entire process of splitting up to a standstill. It becomes a matter of principle to get the mobile phone or the stereo and not let the other person get away with these items. Tempers flare and the scenario becomes distinctly unpleasant.

If this is the case during your split-up you may want to reassess your priorities. Is it really worth spending all this time on quarrelling over possessions? How badly do you want to leave this relationship? Is there a reasonable chance that you will be able to replace these possessions in a year's time if you leave them behind now?

Sometimes it can be useful to bring in a third person to mediate between the two of you and to ensure that a negotiation takes place rather than a battle. Rather than call in someone else, however, it would be good if you could try to sit down and make a list of items you think you should have and then compare your two respective lists. You will hopefully be able to agree on at least some items and can then concentrate on negotiating over possessions of greater importance, and with a bit of give and take you should in the end be left with only a handful of 'difficult' objects. It is helpful if you can be systematic about dividing up possessions because this will hold emotions at bay. In case of doubt it is always easier on your nerves to give up an item. It is not the person who comes out of the relationship with the most items who is the winner; it is the person whose nerves are still intact that scores. Try not to become petty, show that you have style. Don't allow a few plates of bone china to drag you down into venomous altercations, it just isn't worth it. Preserve your strength. You are going to need it for more important things once you are on your own.

Staying friends or not?

Once all the possessions are divided up and the split-up has been announced officially, there is only one more decision to be made: are you two going to keep seeing one another on a social level? In other words, is it possible to reduce a hot relationship to a lukewarm one?

The answer depends on whether you are the one who wanted to end the relationship or whether you are the one who is left behind. If both partners agree that separating is the best thing to do, it may very well be feasible to remain friends. Equally, if you are the one who initiated the break-up, you were obviously discontent with the way things went in the relationship, but you may well feel that, on a less intimate level, you would like to remain in touch with your ex-partner.

The decision becomes more complicated when you are the one who is left behind, in which case you are likely to feel one of two emotions more or less strongly. You are either livid or you are desperate. Some people are mainly angry, with occasional bouts of despair; others are mainly depressed.

When you are mainly enraged, the decision is obvious. You never want to meet him again in your life except to see him getting run over by an articulated lorry, and you certainly have no intention of staying friends. You'll find the mere thought of it insulting ('We'll see whether this new floozy of his is going to type his thesis for him!'). Who does he think he is? If he doesn't want you, then you *certainly* don't want *him*! Fine, problem solved.

But what if you are griefstricken and desperate for him to come back? Should you agree to his proposal to remain in contact? Think about it carefully.

Diane had agreed to such a proposal. Her boyfriend had left her because he had felt fenced in in their relationship and now wanted to go out and do whatever he pleased whenever he pleased, but still keep in touch with Diane, taking her out for an occasional meal to catch up on the latest news. Diane didn't want him to go and felt desolate at the prospect of suddenly being on her own again, so she agreed to the arrangement.

When she saw Martin again after a few weeks, she felt very nervous. She had made up very carefully and was wearing her best clothes. Maybe she could win him back; maybe he would realize what he missed. They went out, and everything went well. They had an animated chat about work and holiday plans. Martin told Diane how he was planning on going on a trip with a friend this summer and how well his new job was going and how he had started going to the theatre again; in short, he was having a marvellous time without her. Diane felt hurt that he had got over their relationship so easily. She decided not to see him again, but when he called a month later, she went out with him once more; at least she was being taken out by a man, even if they weren't a couple any more.

This time, she felt even more nervous than the first time, hoping that he would give her some sort of sign that he still cared for her, but to her great disappointment, their meeting was just as lighthearted and non-committal as the previous one. When she got home that evening she felt utterly miserable and dejected. She realized that she could not handle seeing Martin on a friendship basis and consequently asked him not to contact her again.

When you are in the process of nursing a wound, it is not a good idea to expose yourself to situations where it is ripped open again and again. When your partner has left you, a lot of disturbing emotions come to the surface: you suffer from partnership-withdrawal symptoms. Every time you see him again it is like going back on the drug and consequently having to go through the agony of the withdrawal symptoms again. Don't put yourself through this ordeal over and over again! It is masochistic and does not achieve anything. Better an agonizing end than endless agony.

Give yourself time to recover from the hurt, allow the wound to heal completely before you expose yourself to any further meetings with your ex. It can take a long time, sometimes years, to pick up the pieces, but that's all right. As long as you are still pining for him you are incapable of entering wholeheartedly into a new relationship, so get the healing process underway as soon as possible.

As a rule of thumb it is probably best to leave the decision of whether to stay friends or not to the person who has been left. Unless both partners are very mature it can be a lot easier for the injured party to recover if the relationship is broken off completely for at least a year.

You know that you are over him when you spot him in the street and don't feel you are going to have a minor heart attack; you know that you are in control when the thought of him does not stir any emotions, neither good nor bad, in you any more.

Emotional problems

The feelings that are described in the following occur during and after the split-up in various forms of strength, depending on your personality and your individual attitude towards the event. At this point I would like to point out quite clearly that if you have these negative feelings *while you are going out with someone*, then you have the wrong man by your side. If the relationship is good you feel happy, so if you get unpleasant feelings all the time while you are with him you might as well split up; at least then you will have a good reason for all the unhappiness.

Going through a separation from someone you have been with for a while is difficult, the more difficult the longer you have been together and the closer you were. Splitting up with your partner is comparable to what people go through emotionally when a person close to them dies, for example grief, loss, anger, guilt and depression. And even though your partner hasn't died, you have still 'lost' him, even though it may have been you who initiated the separation.

Guilt

It keeps you awake at night and it mars your days: guilt. You told him that you want out of the relationship and he got really upset. You feel callous and selfish for inflicting all this pain. He reminds you of all the good times you have had together, all the things he has ever done for you, and you begin to feel ungrateful and start wondering whether you are being too fussy. You find it unbearable to see the hurt in his face, and at that moment all you want to do is put your arms around him and tell him that you are going to stay. *Please don't do it.* If you do, it would be a big mistake and even more cruel than leaving him. If you could you would make it easier on him but you can't. The way he reacts to your leaving depends on his personality, and there is nothing you can do about his personality. It is not your fault that he takes it so hard.

If you give in to your feelings of guilt and tell him you'll stay you are doing more damage than good. Giving in because you feel sorry for him only solves the short-term problem of alleviating his momentary distress, but you are still stuck with all the problems that made you want to leave him in the first place.

Some couples split up and get together on this guilt-yoyo time and time again, and it goes on until one party gets so fed up that they refuse to play the game any more. If you are in such a situation then ask yourself whether you are only staying out of pity or because you cannot stand being the 'baddy'. Neither reason is good enough and will only result in you going back until you start hating your partner.

If you must go back, never go back under the same conditions. Things are not working out as they are, so rules have to be changed. But even with you imposing new conditions on the relationship, chances of success are slim. A good relationship works well automatically, and even though there may be points of irritation, they are minor and are easily offset by the positive aspects. You need to agree naturally on the major aspects of your relationship, and this cannot be forced by agreements. If the partners are incompatible, there is no point in staying together.

Women have a curious ability of stabbing themselves in the back. They get fed up with their man's bad behaviour, they suffer in silence or noisily and finally decide that they want no more of it. They say so, but when confronted with a distressed partner they immediately start feeling guilty and looking for explanations for his unacceptable behaviour, like, 'He can't help putting me down all the time, his mother did the same to him,' or, 'He has to have an affair, I'm just not that good in bed,' or, 'He is lazy because he wasn't taught how to fend for himself when he was little.' This is all well and good, but it doesn't alter the fact that his behaviour makes you unhappy, and at this point it is not in your interest to play devil's advocate and try to explain away his shortcomings. You cannot be plaintiff and counsel for the defence at the same time.

Stand by your decision to leave and see it through. If you have told your partner what it is that bothers you, you have given him the chance of doing something about it. It is not your duty, however, to volunteer as his emotional guineapig and hang around until he has learned to change his ways. That is the job of a psychotherapist. They are getting paid for it.

Guilt can also be induced from the outside. Other people may tell you how sorry they feel for your ex and how hard he is taking the whole thing. Or your boyfriend himself may tell you that you are ungrateful and cold and that you will never find anyone who can meet your exaggerated standards. In extreme cases he may even threaten to kill himself unless you come back. What he is telling you is that your behaviour is unreasonable, cruel and inhuman. You are a monster. So why does he want you back?

What is happening here is emotional blackmail, a form of manipulation that has the sole purpose of getting the blackmailer what he wants. If someone accuses you of selfishness by pointing out how they are suffering, they are at least as selfish as you are, so you are quits. Of course you should not take threats of suicide lightly. It is obvious that your partner needs massive support now, and it would certainly be appropriate to alarm some of his friends and ask them to look after him for a while. You may also feel you need to stay in touch with him over the phone for a period of time, ringing him regularly first and later less frequently until he has got over the worst. There is, however, no point in going back to him. All this would achieve is that you would eventually start hating him because he holds that Damocles sword of suicide over your head every time you make a move away from him.

Guilt is a destructive feeling that is confusing and unhelpful in that it blurs the real issue. You have to take responsibility for your decisions, and it is possible that your decision causes distress to someone else, but there is no point in staying if it makes you unhappy. You have a responsibility towards yourself. You have to see to it that you are happy, because if you are unhappy you cannot make anyone else happy, so in the long run it is better for everyone concerned if you look after yourself. If you stay when you want to go you become resentful, and that is not going to be good for the relationship or for your partner.

Hoping against hope

It is said that hope dies last, and this is certainly true for relationships. It is hope that keeps a hopeless relationship going; it is hope that prolongs the agony of getting over a partner who has left you. No matter how unpleasant his behaviour, you hope he will change one day; no matter how clearly he told you or demonstrated that he doesn't want to be with you any longer, you keep on clinging to that straw of hope that he might change his mind.

Hope is a powerful tool in your emotional armoury, but it depends heavily on the state of mind it is linked to whether you can use it to your advantage. When hope is coupled with despair it is often unrealistic and unsuccessful in achieving what you want to achieve; if, however, hope goes hand in hand with a relaxed and confident attitude, it often leads to the fulfilment of your expectations, albeit in a different way than you had foreseen.

Let me give you an example. Let us assume your boyfriend has left you. He has moved out, you have his new address and telephone number and he has offered his continued support and friendship should you want it. You have still not recovered from the shock of separation, you are desperately lonely and want him back at all costs, so you ring him every day, asking his advice, telling him about your day, asking him to come over for dinner, and asking him to come back. He gives you the advice you asked for, he listens to your account of your day, he declines all invitations to dinner and assures you that he won't come back. You are desperate. You were hoping that through your increased efforts he would realize what he was missing but it doesn't seem to work. Even though you are making valid attempts at winning him back, he stands by his decision. The more unmovable he proves to be, the more desperate you get. You are now creating a catch-22 situation for yourself. Your increased efforts to be helpful and convincing become indirectly proportional to his tendency to withdraw; in other words, the more you try the less he responds and the more distressed you get.

It is a very different situation if hope is coupled with confidence. The situation can be the same. He has left you and now lives somewhere else. You feel lonely so you arrange to see your friends frequently. Sometimes you need to ring him when there are matters that need sorting out that concern the two of you. You are friendly and polite; after all, you had some good times together, You can handle these conversations with style (albeit with some trepidation) because you hold the hope that one day you will have a good man by your side, whether it is your ex *or somebody else.* Your hope for happiness is less rigid than that of the desperate person. You are not telling fate *how* to make you happy, you are just expecting to *be* happy again. This attitude creates a feeling of cheerful expectation which in turn makes you feel and look more contented, and it is that look of cheerfulness that attracts other people to you, and one of these other people may be a future boyfriend. If you don't get what you want it just means something better is on its way to you. This applies to houses, jobs, and everything else, including boy-friends.

Once a relationship has officially split up, it is understandable that one or both of the partners should entertain hopes that the separation is only temporary. If, however, the split-up goes back more than a year and you still cannot stop yourself from ringing him and trying to see him in the hope that he will come back, even though he is already with someone else, your problem may be greater than you think. When your ex has gone into a new relationship, then he is giving you and everyone else a sign that he has made a decision, and this decision is not in your favour. If you still insist on running after him you have somehow lost touch with reality; you are deluding yourself. But why do you do it? Why do you have this overwhelming need to win back this particular man?

Usually the answer lies somewhere in your past. Women who cannot let go of their ex often suffer from lack of self-confidence and self-esteem, having been brought up in a tradition where a woman's worth is determined by the man she goes out with or is married to. Once you take the man away there is precious little left in the way of self-worth. Another reason for clinging onto a man can lie in the fact that, during this particular relationship, your partner has eroded your confidence through constant criticism or ridicule, and now you are stuck with a low opinion of yourself.

When I come across a case like this in my practice, I will first of all take my client through a brief psychoanalysis to determine what happened in their life to make them feel so worthless, and once we have discovered the reason and worked through it, I can proceed to help the client build up self-confidence.

If you feel you cannot get to grips with the separation from your partner, it may be useful to seek professional help. Sometimes it is difficult to sort out a problem by yourself because you are simply too close to it. An experienced counsellor or therapist will help you see your situation from a different angle which in turn makes it possible for you to adopt a more positive attitude.

Anger

When a relationship is about to end, there is always tension in the air. You can feel something is wrong, you are alarmed, you start asking questions, your partner is evasive and you get into a row. Or you both are dissatisfied with the way the relationship is going and start nagging one another about your various shortcomings, and before you know it, you are into a slanging match of major proportions. When the relationship finally splits up, the original tension begins to fade. Thank God you won't have to put up with his snoring and his uncooperative attitude concerning house-work any more! But as the original tension dissolves, a new tension begins to build up, and with it a new bout of anger which I call the post-mortem anger.

Post-mortem anger occurs whether your split-up was traumatic or amicable, and it is in the latter case that it may come as a surprise. What happens is that you begin to go over the relationship in great detail, with a fine-tooth comb so to speak, remembering all those incidents which seemed insignificant at the time but now, with hindsight, suddenly take on a new meaning. You are hurt and therefore you begin to gather 'evidence' for his shortcomings, and you usually don't have any problems finding examples; in fact, the more you think about it the more instances you remember – and the angrier you get.

44

How could you endure it for so long? Why couldn't he make more of an effort? Did the relationship mean so little to him? His forgetting your birthday that one time begins to assume alarming proportions as you think back at it, even though you both laughed about it at the time. His never giving you little surprises or treats now seems a clear sign that he didn't care, whereas at the time it only seemed a minor irritant. You dissect his behaviours and attitudes from day one of the relationship, picking out all the negative bits and getting annoyed over them. Even though you may have ended the relationship yourself, you are still angry at him for having behaved in a way that forced you to walk out.

But the anger is not only directed towards him, it is also aimed at yourself. As you are examining all his shortcomings, you cannot help but ask yourself why you didn't do something about them at the time. The answer is that at the time, on the whole, you were contented with the relationship and could therefore afford to accept minor flaws, whereas now you feel rejected and unhappy which is making you petty.

Monica had just split up with John, her boyfriend of four years. There had been a lot of quarrelling in the relationship over the years. John had ardently pursued Monica to start off with, but as soon as they had had sex for the first time, his enthusiasm cooled off. He was no longer attentive or loving, so Monica told him to get out of her life. This rebuff rekindled his interest in her and he started pursuing her again, until they ended in bed once again. Monica made it very clear what she expected of John and told him in no uncertain terms that she was not going to put up with him using her as a sexual plaything, and John pulled himself together for a while, but soon the old pattern emerged again. It seemed that he could only be loving and attentive when she was cool and distant. As soon as she showed feelings for him, he in turn became cool and remote. They seemed unable to find a common denominator emotionally.

They split up several times during those four years but always got back together because of John's perseverance. After each split-up, Monica experienced great feelings of anger, both at John and at herself. On the one hand she could see quite clearly what was happening, but on the other hand she felt unable to ultimately resist John's promises. With every time her hopes were shattered she became more determined to split up for good, but it took five attempts until she finally succeeded. At that stage, she felt she was about to lose all self-respect if she permitted herself to fall for John's promises yet again. Monica's anger at herself was so powerful in the end that she managed to leave John for good.

You know that the worst is over when you start having fantasies of revenge. These can range from finding him sitting in a pub all by himself, smoking like a chimney, drinking too much and *deeply* regretting that he lost you through his own stupidity, to bumping into him when you are wearing a slinky little number, looking your best and with a gorgeous hunk on your arm. These daytime reveries announce that you have reached the peak of your post-mortem anger and that you are now on your way to recovery. The fantasies make you feel better because they are at the (imagined) expense of your ex. You are now beginning to get away from self-pity and switching into a more active mode again.

Anger at your partner and at yourself is a natural phenomenon that occurs to a greater or lesser extent to everyone involved in a split-up. It is a useful, if at times unpleasant, emotion to experience because it helps propel the process of separation forward and helps bring about change more quickly. Where anger is entirely absent it is either repressed (see page 52 on depression) or the person was not emotionally involved in the relationship.

Inferiority complex

This is another emotional problem many women struggle with when their relationship with a man has come to an end: they feel ugly and stupid and spend a lot of time criticizing their looks, their intellect and their abilities. The subconscious reasoning that accompanies this inferiority complex is as follows, 'If I was as goodlooking as I thought, he wouldn't have left me'; or, 'If I was clever enough to discuss his job with him, then he would have given me more attention and I wouldn't have felt so angry at him and left him.' In other words, you are making a shortcoming in yourself responsible for his lack of interest. You are looking for a flaw in yourself to justify his bad behaviour. You are walking down the streets looking at all the other women who seem so much prettier than you; you are listlessly attending parties, listening to some other women's clever conversation, feeling totally frustrated at your own inadequacies. There is no doubt in your mind that you don't stand a chance of ever luring a man into your net because you are so blatantly unattractive – or are you?

Let's just think this through logically. So you are ugly, stupid and uninteresting; these are the facts. Now think back to the beginning of the relationship with your ex. How did it all start? Did you have to grab him by the scruff of his neck and drag him off into your bed? No? So he must have come on his first date out of his own free will, right? He even *continued* seeing you after the first date although he could have taken the opportunity to quietly disappear.

Fine. Now, how can we explain all this? There are two possibilities: either the man was a complete idiot not to notice that you are ugly, dumb and uninteresting, or you are not as ugly, stupid and boring as you think. If he is an idiot then you can only congratulate yourself on finally having got rid of him (remember your standards!), and if you conclude that you cannot be all that unattractive as you think then surely you can brighten up and look forward to a new relationship with someone else!

We tend to become supercritical of ourselves when we are under stress. Splitting up creates tension; in fact *any* change in life, be it good or bad, creates tension, and the more tension we are under the greater our tendency to unrealistic self-doubts.

Please note that self-doubt is not the same thing as self-assessment. Putting yourself down is detrimental to your emotional wellbeing, whereas assessing yourself critically is an entirely different matter. It is good to look at yourself and examine where you went wrong in the past, provided you use this information to change the things you don't like about yourself. It is, however, unconstructive to use that same information to give yourself a hard time. This doesn't achieve anything, and it will only depress you which is the last thing you want in your present situation.

When you have just come out of a traumatic separation you

want to do everything you can to cheer yourself up. The less time you spend brooding the better. This is *not* the time for self-accusations or painstaking soul-searching; you just won't do yourself justice.

Odds are that you are not as useless as you think and that your ex is not quite as wonderful as you thought. Let all the aggravation boil down before you make major judgements about yourself or your ex-partner; there is plenty of time for that later.

Besides, if you are really worried about your looks, this is the time to do something about them. Try out a new hairstyle, go on a make-up course, buy some new clothes. If you feel your education could be improved, get on a course, start getting involved in a subject matter you are interested in, start reading the newspapers regularly to be informed. If something bothers you about yourself, the best strategy is *to do something about it straight away.*

Even though you may not be able to influence all aspects of yourself, you can certainly change a great deal. With a bit of initiative, you can use your time on your own to create self-confidence and a positive outlook on life, and that in itself will make you more attractive, to yourself and others. Self-pity or self-development: the choice is always yours.

Loneliness

One of the main fears about splitting up is the prospect of suddenly being on your own again. Where there was company before when you were watching television, eating a meal, sleeping or going out, suddenly there is a void. Being on your own is not a problem as long as you know your partner is going to be back eventually, but once you have parted company, this possibility is ruled out; you know that, for the time being, you are going to be alone.

The fear of loneliness and the inability to be on your own are the main reasons why bad relationships are upheld, despite the fact that they have obviously turned sour. Some women are hooked on a sense of security and prefer to stay in a bad relationship rather than face an unknown future on their own. The problems of the relationship still seem better than the pain of loneliness.

Whereas once it was nice to have time to yourself while your man was away on business, now you feel deserted and isolated. He has left, and he has left a gap in your life. Everything around you reminds you of him. You may still have some of his things lying about in your flat, and every time you look at them they jolt you back into painful memories. You have lost the person who was closest to you and at the same time you are also badly shaken by conflicting feelings such as anger, grief and depression about that very person. It doesn't rain but it pours. . . .

And yet, being on your own after a separation is also a necessary process. It helps you work through and get over a relationship that had to end for one reason or another. Even though you may feel lonely, the worst possible thing that could happen at this stage is for you to go straight into another relationship. If you did, you would leave unfinished grieving business behind which would later only end up encumbering your new relationship.

Loneliness after a separation is part and parcel of emotionally digesting the trauma. This does not mean that you need to sit at home, moping. It is at a time like this when you need your friends most, so that at least you are not on your own all the time. Hopefully you will not have neglected your friends while you were with your partner because now you need a sympathetic ear to pour out your troubles to.

Apart from talking to your friends, it is also a good idea to pamper yourself a little, treat yourself to baths by candlelight and gourmet meals. Start changing things round in your flat so that they are the way *you* want them; collect all his things and have them sent to his place (no need to have stabs of agony every time you see his clock which you never liked anyway). Fill your diary with as many social events as possible to keep your spirits up; there is enough time left to be on your own and think about the past when you get home after the parties. Flirt as much as you like, compliments are just what you need right now, they are balm to the wounded ego, but get over the old relationship first before you embark on a new one. You will see how you are gradually getting back to your old self where you can enjoy life again and be happy and relaxed. And before you know it, new opportunities arise, new friendships develop and you are busy dating again. . . .

49

Cynicism

Your present relationship may not be the first one that ended in separation for you. Throughout the years, there may have been a succession of lovers and boyfriends, but nothing that lasted; either you were keen on someone who wasn't very interested in the relationship, or he was chasing you, but your heart wasn't in it. Once you have been through a few break-ups, you may feel that exasperation is beginning to set in. Will you *ever* get it right? *Is* there the right partner for you somewhere out there, or are *all* men useless?

It is at this point that you may be tempted to slip off into cynicism. Watch out for thoughts like, 'I don't think I'll bother, men are all the same,' or, 'Men are just incapable of having a meaningful relationship, they just don't care,' and so on. It is unlikely that your generalizations are correct. Just as there are men who are genuinely looking for a lasting relationship, there are also women who find it impossible to be faithful to one man.

Cynicism, however, is one way of building a protective wall around you that is designed to prevent you from getting hurt again. The logic behind this is that if you just give up and refuse to get involved, you can't get hurt. Or so you think.

Being cynical will certainly do the trick to keep men away – bitterness and sarcasm put people off. So your protective wall keeps men out, but at the same time it also becomes your prison: the wall prevents you from moving about freely, and your view is restricted. You have decided that the world outside is hostile and you won't play any longer. It is up to the men to convince you that they *really, really* want you; otherwise you won't come out. Unfortunately this strategy does not work, because seeing the wall puts other people off in the first place, so they won't even try to get close to you.

Rather than being cynical, try to be constructive and start thinking about the reasons why there is this pattern of constant failure in your relationships. Let us just assume for a moment that it is not *only* the men's fault. Is it possible that you have a problem with your attitude whenever you are in a relationship? Let me give you an example.

Susan had been in a number of relationships, none of which

had worked out. Some of these relationships had been very promising, as Susan had to acknowledge, but she still ended up with the men walking out on her, with two of them already at a stage where marriage had been discussed. Susan was on the verge of giving up; her view of men had become very unfavourable indeed. However, she had decided that she wanted to know why the same pattern kept repeating itself over and over again, and whether there was anything she could do to improve her situation.

When we looked into her past relationships it turned out that Susan was full of enthusiasm when she started off with a new boyfriend, to an extent where she put him on a pedestal. As time went by, however, she began to find fault with him, feeling disappointed at his weaknesses. To her, his occasional inattentions and shortcomings were a sign that he was losing interest in their relationship, so she started getting querulous and bitter with him. As her despair at his supposed inattentions grew, the relationship started deteriorating. Susan was in a bad mood most of the time, accusing her partner of inconsideration over every little thing he did wrong. In the end, her partner was either so fed up that he walked out, or she lost all respect for him and left him.

This pattern seemed to suggest that Susan *expected* her relationships to go wrong, and her behaviour was certainly promoting a future split-up. Her initial enthusiasm appeared just as unrealistic as her later criticism of her partner.

When we looked back at Susan's childhood under hypnosis, it became apparent where the problem lay. Susan had adored her father, a charismatic man who spent a lot of time with her over the first ten years of her life. Then, suddenly, he seemed to turn away from her, no longer interested in what she was doing and no longer available to talk with her about her problems. It later turned out that her father was having an affair, and soon after, he left his family temporarily to live with his mistress. Susan's mother felt bitter at being left with two children to look after, and even though the father returned after a while, things were never the same again. Susan's mother reproached her husband openly for having abandoned her, and there were countless rows over the years, until the upset had finally died down, but Susan felt she had never got over the disappointment of her father dropping her like that.

So here we had the explanation for Susan's behaviour; history was repeating itself. Even though she remembered what had occurred during her childhood, she hadn't realized that she had consequently gone through life expecting the same thing to happen again. Once she had become aware of the link between past trauma and present behaviour, she was able to look at men from a different angle. Her outlook became more realistic and her attitude more positive, which helped her with her next relationship. Susan is now happily married.

Depression

Just like cynicism, depression is a form of self-protection. When the world seems too frightening a place to live in, withdrawing into your own shell seems a viable alternative, and it is certainly understandable if you do so when you have just parted from someone who you were close to. Usually, you feel listless and in no mood to join in social events, and after a separation, it can be a good idea to withdraw for a while and lick your wounds in private.

It is important to mourn your loss in order to eventually get over it. It will depend on your personality how long it takes you to be back to your old self, and there is certainly no hard and fast rule what period of time is 'normal' for recovery. However, you should be over the worst within a year, even though you may not be over him altogether. Life gets easier as you go along and the bouts of depression become less frequent and less severe as time goes by. It is really just a matter of sitting it out and employing a few useful strategies (see Chapter 5) to help you through the interim period.

As depression is quite a common phenomenon after a split-up, it is difficult to determine at which point it ceases to be a reasonable side-effect of your present circumstances and becomes a threat to your emotional equilibrium. As a rule of thumb you can say that if you feel under unbearable pressure and are unable to work, even though you may not be suicidal, you should seek professional help to get you through the worst. You have a responsibility towards yourself, and it is a sign of strength rather than weakness to get expert help when you feel you are stuck. That doesn't make you into a mental case; on the contrary, it shows that you are grown-up and mature enough to tell when you cannot cope on your own any more. There are times in our lives where we need to let others help us overcome problems, and that is quite all right.

Depression is anger turned inside instead of out. If you suppress annoyance and discontent, tension builds up inside. Because you are not venting the tension, it begins to accumulate and makes you feel out of control and utterly miserable. Classical symptoms of depression are not wanting to go out, avoiding social contact as far as possible and just wanting to draw the curtains, crawl into bed and pull the covers over you so you don't have to see or hear anything. When you are depressed you are fearful of everything and anything and unable to withstand the slightest stress. Driving your car from A to B sends you into a cold sweat and any upset of your daily routine becomes a major stumbling block. All you want to do is sleep or doze and cut off any communication with the outside world.

As you do everything to avoid stress when you are depressed, you quickly lose your sense of proportion. Tasks that before you could do without thinking twice now become impossible to do. It is comparable to a situation where you haven't used your legs for a month: the muscles become weak and it is painful to start walking again. But because it is painful, you don't want to exercise the muscles, and so a vicious circle is set into motion.

The same is the case with depression. Because you got badly hurt, you withdraw into your shell. After a while you begin to lose touch with the outside world and the outside world with you. Slowly, friends start giving up asking you out or trying to cheer you up because you put them off or even refuse to see them. You sink deeper into depression because now you are really alone. All the while you are burdened with feelings of anger at your ex that you may find disturbing. Anger, guilt and depression go hand in hand, and it is guilt that prevents anger coming to the surface where it belongs.

Maybe you have been taught that it is not 'nice' to be angry at someone, that you should look for faults in yourself rather than in others (see page 44 on anger), and now you are stuck with a lot of negative feelings and nowhere to get rid of them.

Chances are that you have not been able to say what you

wanted in your relationship either. Being nice and accommodating is not necessarily the way to your partner's heart. Often, being agreeable is just an excuse for being unable to say 'no', and if you are incapable of telling your partner what it is that bothers you, he must assume that everything is all right *because he cannot read your mind*. After a while the aggravation builds up to an extent where you either explode or have a nervous breakdown, neither of which is pleasant or solves the original problem.

Do yourself a favour and sort out your feelings. Let someone help you who knows what they are doing. You can achieve very good results within a short period of time. Nowadays there are short therapies available that help you to get the depression sorted out in under twenty sessions, and the benefits you gain will not only help you get over your past relationship more easily, they will also boost your self-confidence and improve life and any future relationships for you. You will also end up liking yourself better, and this will be reflected back to you by others treating you with more respect.

5

Phase IV: Getting Over It

This fourth phase differs from the other three in that it allows you a maximum of control. During decision-making, revelation and the actual split-up, there are a great number of imponderables simply because there are *two* of you involved in the various processes. Once you have actually separated, however, your attention can be focused entirely on yourself and your needs, and this makes it easier to implement specific strategies to overcome the after-effects of splitting up.

The following sections address a number of ways in which you can constructively deal with this last and probably most important phase. You will find step-by-step guides which are designed to give you insight, ideas and practical advice on how to deal with mixed emotional feelings and how to reorganize yourself and your life in order to get over the split-up in a positive manner.

Taking stock

As you are sitting in your flat, on your own, it is slowly beginning to sink in that you are really and truly solo again. You look around you and everything is the same, and yet it seems different, now that you are looking at it from a different situation. The TV set needs to be repaired and he was going to call the engineers in, but of course, now he is gone you will have to attend to it yourself. He used to deal with all matters concerning insurance, and now you are getting a letter saying you still owe money. You have no idea whether he has paid the money or not, so you will have to look into this matter. You look at your diary and suddenly notice all those free weekends which previously you would have filled with a cosy lie-in and a walk in the countryside, but those days are gone. It is good to have time to yourself again, and there have been times when you would have wished for it, but now it seems the situation has gone a bit over the top. You are suddenly faced with lots of changes, and not all of them are good ones.

Step 1: Accept new responsibilities

When you find yourself stranded with that broken-down television set and correspondence about insurance matters that are alien to you, you can do one of two things. You can either throw your hands up in the air and despair at the injustice of fate, or you can accept that you will have to deal with a few new matters that had not concerned you in the past. Out of the two options, the second one is not only more practical but also quicker.

If you are really at a loss as to the best way of dealing with the situation, get on the phone to someone who might be able to help or give advice. This could be a friend, a colleague or a professional organization. You will see that people are willing to give you help and advice, *provided you ask for it.*

The main point is that you accept the fact that it is now up to you to sort things out, be it the removal of an unwanted sofa, the repair of your car or legal advice on insurance matters. Problems don't go away just because you ignore them. Take the bull by the horns and put yourself in control of your life. The sooner you acknowledge these new responsibilities, the sooner you can get any problems sorted out.

Step 2: Ascertain the status quo

In order to get an idea of the number of matters you have to attend to, it can be helpful to draw up two lists: one for administrative matters, and a second one for personal things. Your first list could, for example, contain items such as getting the central heating fixed, organizing for a friend to help you collect the new armchair, putting out a note to the milkman that you want less milk now, and so on. Make sure you list everything, not just the big things. In the confusion of seeing yourself confronted with unfamiliar tasks it is easy to forget the more obvious things. On the personal side, think first of all about the areas of your life that have changed for the worse. Do you feel lonely, bored or restless? Now is the time to dig deep into your long-lost dreams. What were the things you swore you would do one day when you had some time to yourself? Well, what a lucky coincidence: that time has now arrived! In your second list, put all the activities that come into your head, no matter how far-out or unlikely they might seem at first glance. Have a good brainstorming session: don't edit, don't dismiss anything, just keep on writing down whatever comes to mind.

The advantage of writing things down, rather than just thinking about them, is that they become more real and therefore more feasible when you see them in black and white. Also, as you work through your first list and begin to tick off the points with which you have dealt, your achievements are more tangible. It is a good feeling to get rid of one problem after the other, and right now you need all the ego-boosting you can get.

Step 3: Take the necessary steps as soon as possible

This is a very important step in the process of stock-taking. Some people never graduate beyond making the list. They delay from one day to the next by telling themselves that they will *definitely* start tackling the problems – tomorrow. For some reason, today is just not a very good day to do it because they feel tired or in a bad mood or listless. The attitude behind this is, 'I will deal with it when I feel better'. This can, however, turn into a vicious circle. At the back of your mind, you are aware that all these tasks are still waiting to be dealt with, and this causes you anxiety and stress. This in turn makes you feel worse and you feel even less inclined to start on your list.

Let's face it: there is just no way you can get rid of your problems unless you start on them. The sooner you start, the sooner you feel better. And please don't wait for the 'right time' – it may never come!

Talking about it

Splitting up is bound to upset your emotional equilibrium to a greater or lesser extent. Your head is buzzing with unanswered questions: your sleep is disrupted, your stomach is suddenly giving you trouble and you are generally feeling out of sync. When your feelings are in turmoil it is difficult to think straight, and this is where other people, preferably friends, come into it.

Talking to someone else about your problem helps you sort it out in your mind. As long as you only *think* about your situation, memories, conclusions and emotions stay hopelessly entangled.

Expressing your thoughts, however, helps clarify the issues and therefore makes it easier to come to terms with what has happened.

Step 1: Accept your feelings

It is perfectly all right for you to be upset about the split-up. Pulling yourself together in the office is fine, but don't try to kid yourself. Having a good cry about it all relieves tension, and you may find that in the beginning, this is happening quite a lot. While you are in the process of doing the housework, you find your mind keeps wandering off into the past and immediately the tears are falling again.

Be honest with yourself; admit to yourself that it hurts and accept that feeling. You are not a weakling just because you get emotional about it. Splitting up is an upsetting event if you cared about your ex, and the fact that you feel distraught about it shows that your emotions are in working order. From a psychological point of view, it would be far more serious if you were unable to show emotions when something upsetting occurs, because the emotion is there and it has to go somewhere. If it cannot go outside, it will stay inside, and this can lead to depression and desperation.

Step 2: Talk to friends

Being able to talk to friends about your situation is a great release, even though it may only be temporary. You may be worried that your friends will get fed up with listening to your tale of woe, but a good friendship should really be able to withstand that strain. Of course you will be going over the same ground again and again, but that is part of resolving all those mixed feelings, and as time passes the negative feelings gradually lose their intensity and fade, and with it your need to talk about them.

Ideally you have several good friends to whom you feel close enough to confide in. That way you can 'distribute' the burden more evenly and avoid overloading one particular friend with your problems.

It is important to get things off your chest, and other people are needed as a sounding board. They may only listen to you, or they may sympathize or give advice, but no matter what they do, they act as a safety structure that you can cling to while you are feeling emotionally unstable. Moral support is invaluable when you feel you have come to the end of your tether.

It is also enlightening to hear what your friends think of your ex and how they assess your present situation. You may be desperately unhappy at his leaving you, when they may see a number of reasons why you might be glad to be rid of him. This in turn can give you the opportunity to look at things from a different angle. Even though your sadness will recur, there will now also be spells where you think about him in less romantic terms, which in turn puts you into an active mode again (see also page 44 on anger).

Step 3: Keep a diary

This is a step that can either be a substitute for talking to friends, or it can run concurrently. Writing down what you have experienced can often act as self-therapy, even though you are not speaking to someone else directly.

The healing quality of writing about your relationships is getting thoughts and feelings out of your mind and outside your head. This process of externalization makes you look closely at what has happened, and in this way you can begin to analyse it. As you are working through the relationship and the split-up, you will find that things begin to fall into place and you begin to see connections and early warning signals that you had over-looked at the time. It is very much like putting together pieces of a jigsaw puzzle.

You could either keep a day-to-day diary about your feelings as they are at the moment as well as all the memories with which you are struggling, or you could decide to begin to roll up the events from the very beginning, as if you were writing a story, starting with how you met, what you felt about him then, how the relationship developed, right through to the time you split up. As the memories of your time with him are haunting you anyway, you might as well use them in a constructive manner to help you out of your unhappy state of mind!

Step 4: If all else fails, see a counsellor

For some women, being in a relationship means one hundred per cent dedication to the partner, to the exclusion of other friends. They sit by the phone to wait for his call. They cancel any other appointments they may have made if he wants to do something that evening, and it is not surprising that their friends don't take kindly to being dismissed like that. Slowly but surely the overdedicated woman isolates herself, either because she is not making any efforts to maintain her friendships, or because her friends give up on her.

This works as long as the man in question is around and is willing to put up with a clingy woman. The tragedy starts, however, when the relationship breaks up. Many men find it difficult to put up with a woman who follows them around all the time, wants to go where they go and gives up all her own interests in order to blend in with their man's life. It is difficult because it is suffocating and deprives the man of any privacy, and this is why men tend to try and leave this type of relationship as soon as the woman's dependency becomes apparent.

Often, women are aware of their obsession with their partner but feel unable to stop themselves, even though they can see their clinginess ruins the relationship. Once they have been left by their partner, they are truly alone. They feel reluctant to contact old friends because they have been neglecting them, or because the friends have predicted this outcome and now it is hard to admit that they were right. In some cases, parents may not be suitable or available to discuss relationship issues with either.

When you are in a situation like this, it can be very helpful to seek professional help from a counsellor or a therapist. You may actually find it easier to speak to a stranger about your problems. It is easier to discuss difficult personal matters with someone who you know you won't ever see again once you leave their practice.

Seeing a therapist is a must if you find yourself falling into the same old pattern of picking the wrong men or destroying your relationships through jealousy and possessiveness. Finding out why you feel so dependent and unconfident and why you feel worthless without a man by your side all the time can be a revelation and can become the basis for constructive change and an altogether more relaxed and positive outlook on life and relationships.

Learning from the past

Even though everything is over, there is always a tendency to reminisce and to go over the past, which in turn evokes all those feelings we discussed earlier in the book. You remember his faults, and you get angry; you remember your own mistakes, and you feel guilty; you start comparing the past with the present, and you feel lonely.

At this point I would like to say quite clearly that *there is no way of preventing these memories from flooding back*. It is therefore futile to attempt to put the whole business out of your mind. The more you try and avoid a thought, the more it is going to haunt you. You may therefore just as well accept it. After all, thinking about the past helps us understand what happened and consequently, using our new-found insight, to learn from it.

So even if we cannot stop upsetting memories from cropping up again and again, we can at least use them constructively.

Step 1: Look for a pattern

When we think back to things that have gone wrong in the past, it becomes easier to see events clearly. With hindsight, we can often make out a pattern that repeated itself throughout the relationship. Let me give you an example to clarify the point. Tom and Anika had one recurring problem in their relationship. They had bought a little house together which they had only been able to afford because it was in a dilapidated state at the time. Now Tom put all his energy into refurbishing it room by room in order to make it habitable. First, Anika supported him in this and helped with decorating and painting, but when the main jobs were done, she got fed up with spending every weekend on the house, especially because the weather was getting warmer and there was a bathing lake nearby. But Tom was not to be persuaded. There was always a grating to be painted, some shelves to be put up or a piece of furniture to be rearranged. After pleading with Tom for a while, Anika gave up, and even though Tom told her to go off on her own, she refused to do so, and instead stayed home and sulked.

Half a year later, Tom bought himself a computer, and the same problem started all over again. He wanted to try out new games, she wanted to go for a walk. He refused to join her, she stayed at home and sulked. Anika's complaints started developing into rows and weeks of sulks, until the strain got to a point where it destroyed the relationship altogether and the couple decided to separate.

Although this was not the only bone of contention in Tom and Anika's relationship, I am citing it here to demonstrate what a pattern looks like.

Patterns evolve naturally as you begin to spend time regularly with another person, and patterns are useful because they save you from renegotiating the same issue over and over again. If both partners have demanding jobs and have to work late, they may decide only to do their entertaining on weekends. Once this rule has been established, arrangements can be made accordingly. Provided both partners think along the same lines, this pattern of keeping weekdays clear is useful to have. If, however, there is discord as to what should happen at any given time, a pattern can become destructive, especially if there is an unwillingness on both sides to reconsider their point of view.

There are positive and negative patterns in relationships. The easiest way to find them is to think in terms of 'Whenever I do X, he does Y', and 'Whenever he does Y, I do Z'. A good pattern, for example, could be that whenever you get upset, he sits with you and reassures you; or whenever he has problems at work, you take the time to talk it through with him. We can speak of a pattern if we can say that this is so *most* of the time. (There will necessarily have to be exceptions to the rule). Make notes on what patterns you can detect, and then proceed to Step 2.

Step 2: Look for your role in the patterns

As you look at the negative patterns more closely, you will notice that both partners are involved in the unproductive way the pattern operates. Going back to Tom and Anika, it becomes quite clear how an unsuccessful pattern is prevented from changing for the better by their uncooperative attitude: Tom refuses to modify the amount of time he spends around the house or with his computer, and Anika does not go ahead with what she would like to do but sulks instead. Both stubbornly insist that they have a right to what they want, so neither of them will give in and thus help ease the tension. For Tom it would have been possible to compromise and invest two or three evenings a week to go out with Anika, and for Anika it would have been possible to go out either by herself or with some friends a few times a week rather than sulk.

When you check your list of negative patterns, spend a moment thinking of whether maybe you have been a bit inflexible in the past and have thereby aggravated a situation unnecessarily.

But it is not just inflexibility that keeps a pattern negative. Similar problems arise when you are indecisive. When you have tried out various approaches to ease a problem you have with your partner and you still can't get any cooperation from him, then you are obviously not suited for one another. Some patterns are so destructive that the only solution is to walk out of the relationship, for example when the man is violent, an alcoholic or a compulsive gambler. It is noble to stand by him for a while and try to help, but the time must come where you have to leave this situation or you will jeopardize your own wellbeing so severely that you become mentally or physically ill. You can only help someone who *wants* help. If your partner refuses to seek help, you have the duty to at least save yourself and interrupt this destructive pattern: you keep on giving him another chance because he pleads with you not to leave him, only to find that a few weeks later, the same thing happens again.

Learn from the past and, next time, don't allow a negative pattern to continue for too long. When you have tried to be flexible and understanding but still haven't encountered a willingness to cooperate, it is time to call it a day. Don't stay in a bad relationship too long next time but get out when it is still relatively easy.

Filling the emptiness

Once he has gone, you are left with a gap. He has taken away his belongings and you have got rid of any reminders you don't want any longer. You are still in the same place, but the place is no longer the same. It is as if you could physically feel an emptiness. Sometimes, in the mornings, when you are still half asleep you may even expect him to come out of the bathroom and drop his wet towel on the bed only to realize that he is not there any longer. But somehow, it is only small solace to know that you have the bathroom all to yourself now, whenever you want. . . .

This feeling of loss is part and parcel of splitting up, and it is therefore helpful if you *can* allow it to be there.

Step 1: Accept emptiness

It stands to reason that you will miss your partner, in spite of any other feelings like anger or disappointment that make you glad he has finally left. But between the bouts of upsetting memories, there are always glimpses of sadness and abandonment and loss.

Allow them to be there. They are part of the healing process. Acknowledge the existence of a feeling of loneliness and be prepared to give in to it occasionally. It is your mind's way of working through the grief of losing someone you once felt very close to.

It is, however, unnecessary to dwell on this feeling constantly. It is there anyway, whether you want it or not, but don't let it stop you from beginning to focus your mind on other matters. There is still enough time for a cry when you are lying in bed in the evening, trying to go to sleep.

Step 2: Fill in the social emptiness

In order to prevent loneliness from ruling your life, you will have to actively counteract it. If you allow emptiness to take over, you prolong the period it takes you to get back to be your 'old self' and enjoy life again.

Create entertainment for yourself. If you have been separated for just a short while, it is important that you have company as often as possible, and this should take preference over what sort of entertainment you seek. There is no point in going to see a weepy film or a romantic play just then; save yourself the pain. Join others in what they are doing and fill your diary as fully as you can. Don't wait for others to make the first move. Invite friends over for a drink (this may be a good opportunity to announce your separation officially), organize a picnic, an evening out to the theatre, a game of squash; get together with good friends on a one-to-one basis to talk (see page 57).

You may well find that you lack the impetus to organize these events right now. *Please don't let that stop you!* Arrange for at least a few things to take place, especially over the weekend. During the week, there is work and there are your colleagues you can talk to, so that you have at least some distraction, even though you may find your mind wandering off every once in a while. This difficulty in concentrating may also pervade your evening at the theatre – but go anyway. Things are not as they were before, be they at home, at work, or in your spare time, and you'll have to accept this sooner or later. Now all events take place minus one important person, and this changes how you feel about yourself and about these events.

The good news is that it is only a phase. As time goes on, you are getting more used to not having your partner around. Please don't spend your time sitting at home and staring at the empty place next to you on the sofa as you are settling down in front of the television; you'll only make it worse for yourself.

Cut down on time for moping and make an effort to get out and about. As the weeks go by you'll catch yourself genuinely laughing at jokes again and beginning to enjoy at least a few things in life once more.

When you go out, make sure you look your best. Take particular care about your appearance at this stage. It is only too easy to neglect yourself ('It doesn't matter. No one will look at me anyway!') because you feel listless and lonely and rejected. And yet, think about it. When you look in the mirror before you leave the house, it gives you a lift when you perceive yourself as well made-up and dressed well, doesn't it? Remember that feeling when you get ready for a party and you have made special efforts to look good: it makes you *feel* good, doesn't it? Well, use that knowledge now. The more attractive you feel, the more attractive you appear to other people, and you need that right now.

Letting yourself go is the easier option, but in the long run you will get through this phase more agreeably if you can make the special effort to look after yourself.

Step 3: Fill in the physical emptiness

When the sexual side of the relationship has been good, you may miss your partner physically more than anything else, and unfortunately there is no easy solution to that problem. Some women find that, once the news of their split-up gets around, a 'volunteer' appears on the doorstep to 'help' you get over the loss, and you may be quite happy to let someone else console you. However, don't forget your standards altogether. Even a casual affair should not be entered too lightly. Apart from the danger of AIDS or other sexually transmitted diseases, you might get hurt by someone who is inconsiderate and uncaring, so switch on your brain before you say 'yes'!

Whatever you do, please don't think this is your new man just because you have slept with him a couple of times. As long as you are not over your last relationship you are not ready for a new one. He may be, but you are not. You have just put one split-up behind you, and unless you want a second one on your hands, please take it easy with your present lover. If you are aware that you need him for the physical comfort *please tell him*; don't let him think that you want a serious relationship.

Don't see him too often – women have a tendency to fall in love once they have slept with a man, and you are not ready for real commitment yet.

Working on new projects

Now is the time to get down to doing all those things you have always wanted to do if only you had a lot more time. . . . Well, here you are: plenty of time, no one to stop you, no one else to consider, you can go straight ahead! The time between relationships is ideal for new projects and self-development, for getting things sorted out, both in your private life and in your job.

The prospect of tackling something all by yourself may well seem daunting at first, but since you don't have much of an alternative, the only way is forward.

Here are some tips to help you on your way.

Step 1: Choose a project
This may prove to be the first major stumbling block. You may feel unable to think of anything at all that you would want to tackle right now because you simply feel too dejected to

contemplate attempting something new. Don't worry, there is a way out of this dilemma. Think of something 'old', a matter which still has to be dealt with but which you have neglected over the last months or years. It could be something you started and never finished, like sorting out your wardrobe or getting rid of a few old things in the loft; or it could be something you promised to do for a friend and never got round to doing, for example finishing off that dress you made for her or helping her with some painting. Basically, look for any unfinished chores that are still lurking at the back of your mind. As you are tidying away your past relationship mentally, you may as well tidy up any other old matters. Many women find it therapeutic to rearrange their place and throw out unwanted stuff. One client told me. 'It feels like I'm throwing him out of my life, together with all the other old junk. It's like making an official statement that a new era is starting, that I'm leaving the past behind and making a fresh start. I've even rearranged the furniture in my flat.'

If you have another battle with your negative feelings, you might as well make them work for you and redirect all that energy towards a positive goal. You may in fact find it quite easy to come up with a few ideas for new things you would like to try out.

Bear in mind that whatever your new project is, *there is no need for it to be useful.* Choose something which appeals to you, which sounds like fun, which is stimulating or absorbing or a challenge. This is the time to search for something which *you* want, and it doesn't matter whether your friends understand or approve of your choice. Other people just don't come into it at this stage. You may want to learn how to swim, learn a foreign language, study for a degree, start up your own business, get into opera, or start a stamp collection. Anything is permissible as long as it's legal and doesn't leave you bankrupt at the end.

Step 2: Divide the project into manageable parts

One reason why people sometimes fail with their new ideas is that they have no concrete plan of action. As they are thinking about their new enterprise, they see it as larger than life, fraught with insurmountable obstacles, so they just give up there and then, before they have even started.

Any new project may appear daunting as long as it is only in your head, so the answer is to get it out of your head and onto a piece of paper. You may be perfectly right in thinking that pursuing your project might not be entirely straightforward, but if you can see clearly the consecutive steps you need to take in order to achieve your aim, then you are not looking at a mountain of problems but only at a chain of minor problems that can be negotiated as you go along.

Let me give you an example. Let us assume you had decided to take A-levels for a couple of subjects in which you are interested. But even though you would love to be able to say that you have those A-levels, you find yourself greatly worried about a number of points. Where do you start finding the right school? Will you be able to study after having been out of school for so many years? Is everyone else going to be younger and quicker on the uptake? Will you be able to see this project through? Will you flunk the exam because of nerves? All these doubts can put you off very quickly.

But there is a better way of dealing with this matter. Let's start breaking it down into small steps.

Taking two A-levels in French and Biology

(1) Look for a school. Look for ads in newspapers, ask at your local college or your library, talk to friends who have been on a similar course, etc.
(2) Get detailed information from at least two schools.
(3) Ask for an interview with someone at the school. Make a list of all queries that you want to clarify with the school before deciding which school to go to, for example, fees, exams, type of people who attend the course, etc.
(4) Enrol.
(5) If you know that you suffer from exam nerves, arrange to attend a self-help group/see a hypnotherapist/attend a relaxation class just before the final exams.
(6) Start on point (1) *now*.

As you look at the list now, the project already appears more orderly and manageable, doesn't it?

As you draw up your list, make sure you always add as your last point the reminder to *start now*. Any list is only as good as the action you take to put it into practice. Procrastination won't make you feel any better about yourself or your project, so get going as soon as possible.

Step 3: Monitor progress at fixed intervals

Once your project is under way, things tend to sort themselves out as you go along. In the case of taking your A-levels, you have other students and teachers around you who are in the same situation, so you'll have help at hand to sort these problems out.

It is a good idea to check your progress every once in a while to see how you are getting on. This is particularly helpful if you find you are encountering problems on your way or if you are not satisfied with the way things are going.

Formulate clearly what the problem is. Be specific. Don't just say, 'I can't cope with the work.' Define exactly what it is that is causing you trouble, for example 'I don't understand this particular chapter' or 'I don't seem to use my time to the best advantage.' By formulating the problem clearly it becomes easier to find a solution. The hazier the query, the more difficult to determine your angle of attack.

Step 4: Anticipate the successful outcome

In this context let me teach you a trick of how to use your subconscious mind to your advantage. It is in your subconscious mind that you hold all the memories of everything that has ever happened to you, of everything you have ever seen, heard or experienced. Accordingly, the subconscious mind also holds our expectations, because what we anticipate to happen next is born out of our experience of what happened last time. So if you failed your driving test last time, you hold a memory of failure in your memory and you expect to fail next time. Because you anticipate failure, you fill your mind with pictures of disasters: you imagine how you overlook a stop sign, how you get flustered, you imagine the examiner shaking his head in disapproval and, of course, all these mental pictures result in your getting nervous in *reality*. You have now preconditioned yourself to fail a second time!

The good news is that this system also works the other way

around. As your subconscious mind cannot distinguish whether you have done something in reality or whether you have just imagined it, you can easily hype yourself up by filling your mind with positive images, for example, about the successful outcome of your project. Set some time aside every day where you relax quietly, just close your eyes and begin to visualize how you receive that certificate for the course you are working for, feeling that elated feeling that you have made it; see yourself having lost that excess weight, standing in front of a mirror in a smaller size dress that fits you perfectly and feel that sense of pride in yourself.

If you visualize the successful outcome regularly, it will help you keep motivated to see your project through to the end and it also makes you feel better generally. Success is good for body and soul, and the more you fill your mind with positive thoughts, the higher is the likelihood of your success images coming true.

Building self-confidence

What I just explained about the subconscious mind also applies to the area of self-confidence. The last relationship memory you have stored is one of failure, no matter whether you left him or he left you, so for most women the first thing that goes after a split-up is their confidence. 'I just can't hold a man', or, 'I always pick the losers', or even, 'I don't think there are any decent men around any more' are all typical thoughts that indicate an attitude of hopelessness and low morale. What better time to start working on yourself than now!

Step 1: Get a clear picture about yourself

Your self-confidence may be good in respect of your job, but you may feel a lack of it when it comes to personal relationships. Some people can act confidently with strangers, but not with friends. Even though a lack of confidence may pervade most areas of your life, it is still important to pinpoint a few major points. Which area of your life would benefit most by improved self-esteem? It is perfectly all right to work on only one area, because once you improve in one area, your confidence will automatically spread over to others; so you might as well select the issue that is closest to your heart.

Talk to a good friend and ask them to tell you how they perceive you. You may be surprised to find that your self-image differs considerably from the image others have of you. Getting a second opinion can be useful because often we are our own worst enemies and much stricter with ourselves than others would ever be, and it can help us get a more balanced perspective to listen to how our friends see us.

Step 2: Learn to relax

A confident attitude comes from a relaxed mind. In order to relax your mind you will have to, first of all, relax your body.

Find yourself a comfortable chair and settle back in it. Put both feet flat on the floor (you may have to take off high-heeled shoes) and make sure your breathing is not restricted by a tight belt. Place your hands loosely on your thighs.

Look straight ahead of you and, without lifting your chin, turn your eyes upwards towards the ceiling, and keep them fixed on one spot on the ceiling. Try not to blink as you stare at that spot. Now wait for your vision to blur, and as soon as it does, let your eyes gently close, take a deep breath and begin to concentrate on how you are sitting in the chair. Feel where your head is, your back, your arms, your hands, your legs and your feet. Take a deep breath.

Now begin to tense the muscles in your feet, hold the tension for a moment and relax them again. As you do so, imagine the muscles in your feet contracting and then smoothing out again as you are letting go of the tension. Then begin to work your way up by tensing and relaxing your legs, your belly and chest area, your hands and arms, and finally your shoulders and face muscles, always remembering to visualize the muscles bunching up and lengthening out again.

Once you have done this, take a deep breath again and spend a few moments on imagining that your entire body is so limp and loose that you feel like a rag doll. Pretend that all energy has left your body. Test this by lifting one hand a few inches off your leg and then let it drop down heavily, imagining that you are now doubling your relaxation. Then do the same thing with the other hand, imagining that you are now going five times deeper.

Now concentrate on your stomach. Picture your stomach

getting warmer and warmer, calmer and calmer, spreading tranquillity throughout your body and mind.

When you are ready, tighten all your muscles at once, and as you let them relax, open your eyes again.

The whole exercise needn't take more than five minutes, and it is highly effective. Practise it twice a day for a couple of weeks and you will be able to reach a pleasant state of relaxation even more quickly by just sitting down, closing your eyes, taking a deep breath and lifting your hands and dropping them loosely into your lap.

Step 3: Say what you want

Many relationships are distorted or destroyed by the fact that one or both partners will not openly speak about their needs, either because they can't or they won't. He suggests going to his Aunt Maude's for the weekend and she says yes although she'd rather spend some time just with him; she arranges to go to the theatre when he would rather watch that football match on television. In each case, one partner feels he or she has lost out.

This is not to say that there should not be a considerable amount of give and take in a relationship or any other partnership, but it is very important to get the balance right. In order for *both* sides to be happy and contented, it is necessary for *both* sides to be able to express what they want. Unless you can do that, the relationship becomes an elaborate guessing game where your partner is left to wonder why you are in a bad mood again.

Sylvia explained during one of her sessions:

> I was just not used to thinking about what I wanted. I have been brought up to put myself last and make it my first concern to listen to what other people want, especially men. So when my husband asked me what I wanted to do, I couldn't really tell him. I was just not sure what I wanted or when I did, I dared not say it. Instead, I started thinking about what *he* would probably like to do; so I suppose I always said what I thought he wanted to hear. Afterwards I felt resentful, though.

This is a typical example of a pseudo-negotiation between

72

partners. The man offers the woman the choice of what to do, for example, on a weekend, and he receives an answer which he must assume is based on the woman's needs and wishes. He then carries out her wish and is utterly confused when she is in a bad mood.

If you can see something of yourself in the above examples, please consider the following:

(1) *Your partner cannot read your mind.*
(2) *Your needs are just as important as anyone else's.*
(3) *You cannot please everyone but you can kill yourself trying.*

(1)   You may think he should know by now what you want and you feel offended that he still has to ask. But isn't it really to his credit that he doesn't automatically assume you always want the same thing? Surely it is only polite to ensure that the other person is still happy with their usual choice.

You may think it is clear what you want, but this is not necessarily so for others. Don't keep him guessing: tell him.

(2)   It is a fallacy to believe that there are certain groups of people whose needs are more important than yours (men/parents/sick people). If, for example, you are looking after your mother who is permanently disabled, then the automatic assumption for many women is that the mother's needs must come first *because she is ill and because she is your mother.* Therefore you don't go out, you do all her shopping and cooking and cleaning for her, you drop those evening classes and you drop your friends. This works for a little while, and then you start getting resentful. Everyone else is out there having a good time and here you are, stuck with your mother because you feel it is your duty. Whenever you go out you feel guilty because you are neglecting her, whenever you stay in, you feel resentful that her illness forces you to do so.

This is not a good situation, neither for you nor for your mother who will sense your resentment, and there is nothing worse than being dependent on someone who is only reluctantly helping.

In this context it is *vital* you should establish a balance between your needs and hers. You have a responsibility not only towards your mother but also towards yourself. If you don't look after your interests, no one else will. Once you have established a pattern which allows you sufficient time to yourself, you will feel happier and more relaxed around your mother, and that is beneficial for everyone involved. When you are unhappy you are no good to anyone, so you might as well make sure you get what you need.

(3)   Contrary to what your mother may have told you, you are not in this world to please other people. Pleasing others is a tricky situation, anyway, because how do you know you're getting it right? You suggest going to a football match to please him and he only says yes to please you when really he hates football. So two people secretly grit their teeth and spend an afternoon on the terraces, making out they are having a good time. Wouldn't you say that this is ridiculous? Well, it is.

So don't say yes when you mean no, just to please someone else. You may think you are doing them a favour when all you are doing is confusing the issue. This goes for private as well as for professional relationships. There is no point in working your fingers to the bone to please your boss because *you* will have to pay for it in the end by getting exhausted or even ill.

Again, it all boils down to the responsibility you have for your own wellbeing. If you don't run your life yourself, someone else is going to run it for you and you will have to like what you get, rather than getting what you like. You have more control than you think, so make sure you are using it constructively.

Step 4: Start with small steps

Don't run before you can walk: start on easier things when you are beginning to build your self-confidence. Even the slightest positive change *is* a change, and a number of small changes constitute progress, just as much as one big change does.

We have a tendency to undervalue small steps of improvement; our attitude is that they 'don't count'. You may have finally plucked up the courage to exchange a few words with your new neighbour, but immediately you think that this was nothing, everyone could have done it, and probably much better than you did.

Please don't forget, though, that you are only beginning to become more confident; in a way you have an invisible learner-plate on your back, so be good to yourself and acknowledge your efforts. You will get better as you go along.

Doing things differently and in a more assertive way may feel strange to start with. It may feel wrong to comment where you haven't commented before, to join in where you stayed aloof before, or to say 'no' where you would once have said 'yes'. It's like trying to write with your other hand all of a sudden: you feel awkward and clumsy, you are slow, and the results are not as good as those you would get had you written with your 'old' hand. But if you *really* put your mind to it, surely your writing with your other hand would improve, *provided you persisted in practising*!

The same is true of other aspects of life. If you keep on pursuing your goal, no matter what it is, you simply cannot fail. That's how you learned to stand up and walk as a baby, that's how you learned to read and write. You've done it before, you can do it again!

Regaining a positive outlook

Life has its ups and downs, and at the moment you may have a tendency to look at the downs with an extra-large magnifying glass, thereby overlooking the fact that the good sides of life still exist. You could see them, if only you shifted your magnifying glass a bit.

When we are unhappy, everything around us seems to be covered with a grey veil of gloom and doom. We suffer from a blinkered vision that only allows selective attention to negative detail. Even the people on the tube all seem ugly somehow. . . .

Step 1: Shift your outlook towards the positive

If it is true that there are good and bad things in life, then this means you have a choice as to which you want to focus on. At the moment, your mind is filled with memories and thoughts of your past relationship; you fret and worry and feel miserable.

As you sit slouched in front of your TV set, staring glumly at the screen, you are permitting yourself to get immersed in the negative side. Instead, try the following experiment.

Make your present negative feelings into sentences and then

follow them by adding 'but fortunately . . .'. Here are some examples:

I feel very lonely without Richard, but fortunately I've been invited to a party tomorrow.

I feel rejected because he left me for another woman, but fortunately I have good friends.

I feel angry that I allowed myself to be stuck in an unrewarding relationship for so long, but fortunately I can now start working on my self-confidence.

Then go and demonstrate the 'fortunately' parts of your life to yourself. Pick up the phone and ring those good friends you have (provided it is still a sociable hour to do so); start thinking about what you are going to wear for that party and who you are going to flirt with; get yourself a couple of newspapers and start looking for interesting courses/trips/jobs that you can pursue because, fortunately, you now have the time to do so.

This method is also known as counting your blessings, and it works admirably!

Step 2: Restrict negative thoughts to particular times

Start taking control of what is going on in your mind. Let me warn you about one thing, though: it is no use trying to *ban* negative thoughts from your mind. The more you try and make them go away, the more they run after you.

The way to deal with unpleasant thoughts is to banish them to certain times of the day; so, for example, you may decide to worry four times a day about your involuntary single status: at 9 am, at 12.30 pm, 4 pm, and 6 pm. So when you catch your mind drifting off into upsetting memories, stop them and tell yourself that you will be thinking about them at the allocated time. When the time comes, do it properly. Stop what you are doing, lean back and start worrying good and proper. If it is an unpleasant memory that keeps coming up in your mind, go through it in great detail. Make sure you remember every single thing that happened then, and go over that memory at least five times from start to finish, as if you were watching an old film. If, on the other hand, you are worried about loneliness and emptiness, go into that aspect of your life in just as much detail. Think about how you are getting grey and old and uninteresting, mooching about the house in your dressing gown all day long, losing all your friends, getting bored and boring, dying an old maid (and try not to laugh as you do so). Half way through these exaggerated thoughts you will notice that you think this is a lot of nonsense.

After you've done your worrying at certain times of day for a while, it becomes a bit of a chore, and as you are getting used to systematically going through your worry-thoughts, they become trite and boring, and that is what makes them ultimately lose their emotional power.

Becoming your own woman

Being your own woman is *not* the same thing as being immaculately dressed and carrying your briefcase to your executive office on the tenth floor of a chrome skyscraper. It can, but it doesn't have to. Being your own person means that you know how to look after yourself, an essential skill if you want to be counted amongst the adult part of the population. As a mature, grown-up woman you are able to handle your emotions constructively most of the time (nobody is perfect!) and ensure that you get most of the things you need in life. This means also that you learn to discern clearly about what is important to you and what isn't. We don't live forever, so we need to select what it is we want to do with our lives, and whatever choice we make should be tailormade to our personal needs without hurting others in the process.

Most women are very proficient in looking after the wellbeing of others but not so good at looking after their own. And yet, you need to live your own life. No amount of regret will make up for the wasted opportunities when you suddenly find you are sixty and realize you have not made the most of your life. Don't let your life be just one big dream of what you are going to do in the future; *now* is the time to start making dreams come true.

Step 1: Take yourself seriously – with a sense of humour

I have already mentioned earlier in the book that it is important to be aware of your own wishes and needs, and that you should ensure that you fulfil your essential needs by making it known, in a kind but firm way, how you wish to be treated.

Moreover, you need to work on your self-development as you go along, taking on new tasks and expanding your horizons. As you push back your limitations you will notice how good you feel about yourself and, above all, how much more in control.

That doesn't mean you have to lose your sense of humour, though. Just because you are striving to better yourself doesn't have to make you into a mirthless swot who works all hours and never goes out. Self-development can be achieved on a variety of levels, either professionally or privately or both.

You have a responsibility towards yourself, and you should make sure you get the best there is. As discussed earlier on, it is not a solution to lower your standards, but as long as you can keep a perspective you may have fun with the second-best thing, be it a job, a lover or a hobby. Just as long as you are aware that this is not really what you want, you might as well have a good time while you are looking for the right job/lover/pastime. The emphasis here is on 'keep looking'. You will know when you have found the right thing because it *feels* right, not just for the first two weeks but for good.

Step 2: Keep flexible

Rules and regulations are hardly ever completely rigid. There is always room for manoeuvring within the boundaries.

There are social rules which we have to follow in order to make it possible for us to live together in comparable harmony, and that is fine. But when it comes to rules concerning your personal life, you have more flexibility. Most of the time we have more of a choice than we care to admit, and it is mostly just laziness or fear of what the neighbours might say that prevents us from adapting general rules to our own specifications.

It appears to be a general rule, for example, that you must be unhappy when you are on your own. This is a lopsided view of reality, just as the assumption that no couple is complete without children or that a relationship is a safeguard against being lonely. Just as there are countless examples that confirm these views, there are at least an equal number of cases which contradict these beliefs. So we are back to square one once again: in the end you will have to be in touch with yourself in order to decide what you want to do at a given point in time. Don't forget that you have a right to change your opinion at any time without having to apologize for it. When you have been running with your head against a brick wall a few times, it makes sense to change direction. This is not being inconsistent, this is just showing self-respect and common sense.

Step 3: Having a good time!

As you go through your days after the split-up, you will notice how, very gradually, the pain begins to subside and wane, and everyday life takes over your thoughts once again. No matter how traumatic the separation, time will guarantee that it wears off. There is no way of predicting exactly how long you will take to get over it. The only thing that is certain is that you will. The pain cannot stay the same over the years. Instead, the experience of the relationship and how it ended becomes an integral part of your life. Hopefully you will have learned something from it and this knowledge leaves you a better and wiser person.

So what do you do while you are waiting for the anguish to abate? Well, as with most situations in life you have at least two options. You can either give in to your negative feelings and let them drag you down, or you can decide to make the best of this emotional interim time and latch on to some pleasant distractions and entertainments. Of course it will be hard to keep your mind on the play you are watching if you go to the theatre, but you will at least have some spells where you can get really absorbed in the performance, and this is extremely valuable because it helps fill your mind with other things than the past relationship. Of course your mind will wander off sometimes while you are attending your Italian classes, but at the same time you will also find that, for some stretches, you actually get wrapped up in what you are doing. While you are intently thinking of one thing you cannot think of another, and that is the effect you want to create at the moment.

Life is too short to waste it on brooding over events that are in the past. Don't fall into that trap! Make sure you have the best possible time, and even if it is still interspersed with occasional flashbacks, it is on the whole the best way of pulling you up out of that deep dark hole.

You are special and you deserve to be happy. Think about all the good times that are just around the corner, think about how you can treat yourself to a better and happier life and act upon your conclusions *now*. You have the choice between optimism and pessimism. Optimism creates happiness, pessimism creates misery. Which one do you prefer?

Summary

Relationships develop and grow, and often they dissolve again after some time. But even when they last, they imply efforts on both sides, compromise and communication. When one relationship comes to an end, it does not mean that this was your last chance. Even if you are seventy-five, there is always another man where that last one came from!

As we develop and gain more experience, we find it easier to understand what we need and want. This can sometimes mean that we realize that we have to leave our present partner and look for someone who more closely meets our needs. The same is true for men, though. The majority of issues raised in this book equally apply to men, even though their emotional make-up appears to differ from ours in many respects.

Splitting up is always hard for both sides, albeit in different ways. The main thing is to never give in to the illusion that we are powerless in the face of adversity. There are lots of things you can do to help yourself get over the split-up and use your newfound understanding in a positive and constructive way. Not only will you learn a lot about yourself, but you will emerge from the experience a happier and wiser person, and this can only help you with your next relationship, which is bound to be just around the corner!

Index